Developing Reading Fluency

Grades 6–8

Written by
Trisha Callella

Editor: Alaska Hults

Illustrator: Ann Iosa

Designer/Production: Mary Gagné/Carmela Murray

Cover Designer: Mary Gagné

Art Director: Tom Cochrane

Project Director: Carolea Williams

Table of Contents

Introduction

Learning to read is a systematic, learned process. Once students can read individual words, they need to learn to put those words together to form sentences. Then, students must learn to read those sentences fluently to comprehend the meaning of each word and the meaning of an entire sentence. Students' reading fluency develops as they learn to break sentences into phrases and to "chunk" words together into phrases as they read. As students read sentences in phrases, they develop better comprehension of each sentence's meaning, read at a faster pace, and read with increased expression and intonation.

Use the lessons in *Developing Reading Fluency* to meet district, state, and national reading standards as you teach students how to develop reading fluency. The first section contains informal assessments you can use to help determine what skills students have mastered, what they are using poorly or inconsistently, and where the skill gaps are in their reading. The remaining sections are arranged sequentially to help you implement fluency modeling, fluency practice by students, and students' application of fluency strategies. Use the activities to help students build upon the skills they learned in the previous section. The final section of the book contains additional instruction to provide intervention for students having difficulties. The book features the following strategies to improve students' reading fluency:

- **Read-Arounds:** Help students learn high-frequency and content words and practice reading text in phrases as they work in small groups.
- **Phrasing Fun:** Guide students as they practice reading words in a sentence chunked by meaning. Then, have them apply this skill to a longer section of related text.
- **Phrased Text:** Have students read paragraphs where the chunked phrases are visually cued. Then, immediately have students reread the same text without the visual cues.
- **Reader's Theater:** Have students work in groups of four to practice rereading a script until they can fluently read their part in front of an audience. Use the performances as a culminating activity to have students apply all the reading strategies they have learned.
- **Intervention Activities:** Use these activities with individuals or small groups to intervene with students who still struggle with reading fluency. These activities enable students to identify and practice expression, intonation, and the natural flow of fluency.

The activities in this book provide students with a variety of reading experiences. The themes and genres included in each section will motivate students to not only read the text but to read with expression, intonation, and a natural flow. Students will build enthusiasm and confidence as they begin to increase their comprehension and as they successfully apply reading strategies to their everyday reading!

Reading fluency is the ability to read with expression, intonation, and a natural flow that sounds like talking. Fluency is not the speed at which one reads. That is the reading rate. A fluent reader does read quickly; however, he or she also focuses on phrased units of meaning. A student may read quickly but may not necessarily be fluent. Students who read too quickly often skip over punctuation. This inhibits comprehension because punctuation helps convey the meaning. Fluent readers have developed automaticity. This means that they have a solid bank of sight words on which they can rely and that are automatic. Fluent readers can then focus their reading on understanding the message rather than decoding the text. Reading is decoding with comprehension. Fluent readers do both. They read without thinking about how they are reading, and they understand what they are reading.

What does a student who lacks fluency sound like?

A student who lacks fluency may sound choppy, robotic, or speedy.

How does repeated oral reading increase fluency?

Research shows that students increase their fluency when they read and reread the same passage aloud several times. The support that teachers give students during oral reading by modeling the text and providing guidance and feedback enhances their fluency development. Using this strategy, students gradually become better readers and their word recognition, speed, accuracy, and fluency all increase as a result. Their comprehension also improves because they are bridging the gap between reading for word recognition and reading for meaning.

Why is it so critical for middle schoolers to read with fluency?

Bad habits can be hard to break. By this time, the student has had at least six years to practice and transfer reading skills and strategies. Any student who is not reading with fluency in middle school is not comprehending the text. This is especially worrisome since the student must comprehend nonfiction text well in order to succeed in other content areas. Implement the activities and strategies included in this book to guide the learner to reading fluently.

How do fluency and phrasing work together?

Phrasing is the link between decoding the meaning of the text and reading the text fluently. Phrasing is how a reader groups words in a sentence. A lack of phrasing results in staccato reading, "word calling," and decoding. A fluent reader reads in phrased chunks that are meaningful. Read the information on page 5 to learn more about phrasing.

Phrasing

A student who reads in phrases reads words in meaningful groups. Phrasing helps a student understand that the text carries meaning. A phrase is a group of words that the reader says together and reads together. The way the words are grouped affects the meaning. This is why phrasing affects reading comprehension.

What does phrasing sound like?

Consider how the same sentence can have different meanings depending on the way the words are grouped, or phrased. It clearly affects the comprehension of what is read. For example:

> Patti Lee is my best friend.
> Patti, Lee is my best friend.

Who is the best friend? It depends on how the sentence is read. In this example, punctuation also affects phrasing.

What causes incorrect phrasing?

A student may read with incorrect phrasing for a number of reasons. First, many students rely too much on phonics. This leads to a dependency on decoding. When students focus on decoding, they neglect the message. They turn into expert "word callers." Incorrect phrasing can also result from a lack of attention to punctuation. Some students ignore punctuation altogether, which will result in incorrect phrasing, affect their fluency, and hurt their comprehension.

What can I do to teach and improve phrasing?

1. Use the activities in this book. They are all researched, teacher-tested, and student-approved, and they will help students experience reading fluency success.
2. Photocopy a story, a student's writing sample, or a poem onto an overhead transparency. As the class reads it together, mark off the phrases using a steady sweep of a transparency marker to visually show the voiced phrases. (The sweep should look like a flattened *u* that extends from the start to the end of the phrase.) This visual-auditory connection benefits those students who are still not reading fluently.
3. Read and reread.
4. Model. Model. Model.
5. Echo read.
6. Make flash cards of common phrases to help students train their eyes to see words in groups rather than as individual words.
7. Tape-record students as they read. Let them listen to improvements they make in phrasing and intonation.
8. Write multisyllabic words on index cards. Have students practice decoding them. Teach strategies of looking for known chunks in words and applying meaning to those chunks. As students become more efficient at breaking down multisyllabic words into meaningful chunks, they are able to focus on the meaning of the words, read more fluently, and comprehend more of what is read.

Getting Started

How to Use This Book

The activities in this book provide fun and easy strategies that will help students develop reading fluency. Getting started is simple.

- Read the Stages of Fluency Development chart on page 7. Then, use the assessments that begin on page 10 to determine students' needs. Read the directions carefully to understand the modifications to traditional informal reading inventories. Use this information to create a plan of action and decide on which skills the whole class, groups of students, and individuals need to focus.

- Use the Fantastic Five Format on page 8 with the whole class, small groups, or individuals. This format provides a guideline for developing reading fluency that will work with any genre. Copy the reproducible, and use it as a "cheat sheet" when you give guided instruction. You will find the format effective in helping you with modeling, teaching, guiding, and transferring phrased and fluent reading to independent reading.

- Refer to the Teacher Tips on page 9 before you begin using the activities in this book. These tips include helpful information that will assist you as you teach all students in your classroom to read fluently and, as a result, improve their comprehension of text.

Fluency Activities and Strategies

The sections of this book have been sequentially arranged for you to first model fluency, then have students practice fluency, and finally have them independently apply their newly learned skills. Each section has an introductory page to help you get started. It includes

- an explanation of how the activities in that section relate to fluency development
- the strategies students will use to complete the activities
- a materials list
- step-by-step directions for preparing and presenting the activities
- an idea for how to vary the activities

Each section opener is followed by a set of fun reproducible reading materials that are designed to excite and motivate students about developing reading fluency. Within each section, the readability of the reproducibles increases in difficulty to provide appropriate reading material for students who read at different levels.

Intervention Activities and Strategies

The Intervention Activities section is designed for students who are struggling with fluency. They need direct, systematic instruction in a one-on-one format where you can instruct at the point of difficulty. These five activities provide that opportunity. Some may also work well in a very small group. The activities are designed for intensive instruction to change bad habits and instill solid strategies for reading fluently.

Stage	What You Observe	What to Teach for Fluency
1	• many miscues • too much emphasis on meaning • storytelling based on pictures • sounds fluent but not reading what is written down • playing "teacher" while reading	• print carries the meaning
2	• tries to match what he or she says with what is written on the page • one-to-one correspondence • finger pointing and "voice pointing" • staccato reading, robotic reading	• phrasing and fluency • focus on meaning • read like talking • high-frequency words • purpose of punctuation
3	• focuses on the meaning of print • may use bookmark • focuses more on print than picture • no longer voice points • laughs, giggles, or comments while reading	• phrasing and fluency • focus on what makes sense and looks right • purpose of punctuation • proper expression and intonation
4	• reads books with more print than pictures • wants to talk about what he or she read • reads like talking with phrasing • reads punctuation with expression • laughs, giggles, or comments while reading	• shades of meaning • making connections
5	• reads and comprehends novels and some nonfiction text • reads with 4- to 5-word phrases that match natural speech • reads punctuation with expression • changes voice for different characters or speakers when reading aloud • laughs, giggles, or comments while reading • reads in phrases both silently and orally	• multisyllabic word decoding for meaningful chunks • fluency in nonfiction text • shades of meaning • making connections • fluent reading with advanced punctuation—broken syllables at ends of lines, hyphens, parentheses
6	• reads and comprehends novels and nonfiction text • reads with 5 or more words in phrases that match natural speech • reads advanced punctuation with proper intonation (hyphens, parentheses, semicolons, split syllables at ends of lines, asides, etc.) • changes voice to match tone of the story (intonation sounds grim, excited, etc.) • changes voice to match characters, setting, surroundings, foreshadowing • laughs, giggles, or comments while reading • makes connections while reading (interacts with the text) • reads nonfiction text fluently	This is a fluent reader. Fluent readers just need further practice on material with increasing vocabulary demands.

Fantastic Five Format

Modeled Fluency

Model reading with fluency so that students understand the text and what they are supposed to learn.

Echo Reading

Read one part. Have students repeat the same part.

Choral Reading

Read together. This prepares students to take over the task of reading.

Independent Fluency

Have students read to you.

Reverse Echo Reading

Have students read to you, and then repeat their phrasing, expression, and fluency. Students have now taken over the task of reading.

Developing Reading Fluency • Gr. 6–8 © 2004 Creative Teaching Press

Teacher Tips

1. Teach students who are struggling with fluency and phrasing in guided reading groups. However, be flexible in your grouping. If you are teaching a fluency strategy, then you can group them together. If you are teaching a comprehension strategy or skill, they should be in a mixed guided reading group. This is especially important for middle school students, since they probably have been grouped with the same struggling students since kindergarten. When this occurs, they do not have any daily models of fluent reading aside from you. They must interact with fluent readers in the class. The activities in this book provide many additional opportunities to make sure that these students work with everyone—not just other struggling readers.

2. When asking students to read aloud in class during science, social studies, or reading, give them time to browse the material first. This helps the struggling student get the whole picture before it is broken down.

3. When asking students to read aloud in class, choose names at random by using a flip-up index card booklet or sticks with the students' names on them. When students are chosen at random, everyone pays attention to all of the reading and the struggling students have a higher level of comprehension.

4. Another important thing to remember is that students naturally want to help one another. When a struggling reader reads aloud for the class, fluent readers commonly "help" by telling the student words or phrases to read. Struggling students are often given significantly less time to solve a reading problem than fluent readers are. Try to eliminate that helping. Instead say, "He (or she) can do it," and wait. When given a chance, students will achieve.

5. Do not invite students to use their finger to track while reading. It is a bad habit that trains the eyes to look at only one word at a time. If a student continuously loses his or her place, tell the student to put his or her finger at the beginning of that line of text and move from line to line.

6. If students use bookmarks, have them hold the bookmark just above the line of print they are reading rather than just under the line. When students use a bookmark under a line of print, the bookmark blocks the next line. This keeps students from reading fluently because they cannot see the ending punctuation to anticipate the intonation and expression needed.

7. Teach your students how you mark the phrases read when they read aloud to you. Have practice sessions where they work with random partners to listen and record phrases the partner reads.

Informal Reading Inventories

This section of the book is dedicated to ongoing individual assessment to determine what a student knows, what is used but confused, and what needs further development in the area of reading. The reading selections will give you the opportunity to monitor growth and guide your instruction based on individual needs. Each selection will tell you the following about the student:

1. ability to decode middle-grade nonfiction reading material (goal: read to learn)
2. the background knowledge prior to reading, which will affect comprehension
3. ability to make specific predictions
4. ability to read phrased chunks of text
5. discrepancy between oral and silent reading comprehension
6. ability to retell
7. ability to sequence
8. ability to respond accurately to comprehension questions

To make the informal reading inventories most beneficial for guiding your instruction, it is very important that they are done in their entirety. If any part is skipped, then your knowledge about the student's reading fluency is incomplete. Future instruction should be strategy based—not level based. Therefore, it is important to know which strategy to teach (e.g., retelling, sequencing, phrasing).

Each reading selection is based on a middle-school reading level. Remember that there is often a discrepancy between a middle school student's ability to comprehend fiction and nonfiction text. Most students comprehend fiction text at least one grade level (usually two) higher than their comprehension level of nonfiction text. Since a goal of middle-school reading is to help students make better use of the nonfiction text they read, the reading selections in this book are more heavily weighted toward nonfiction text.

Forms A and B focus on late fifth-grade/early sixth-grade reading level, while Forms C and D focus on later seventh-grade/early eighth-grade reading level. This gives you the opportunity to assess and reassess a student appropriately.

Scoring Goals

Average middle-grade oral reading rates:
(in words correctly read per minute)

%ile	Fall	Winter	Spring
75	126	143	151
50	105	118	128
25	77	93	100

Comprehension questions: grades 6–8

Retelling: sequenced, oral, and silent, 70% of what was read

Sequencing: beginning to end

Goal for students in phrasing: 3- to 5-word phrases depending on meaningful chunking

Directions for administering the Informal Reading Inventory to one student:

1. In advance, photocopy the student text version of the form you choose from pages 13 and 14. Cut along the dotted lines so the student only sees the text he or she will read. Get a timer.

2. Ask the student the background knowledge questions. Quickly take notes on his or her responses.

3. Tell the student the title of the reading selection. Tell him or her that the background questions are related. Ask the student to make a prediction. Write down what he or she says. (Watch for students who simply rephrase the title. That is not a prediction and indicates a need for direct instruction in making predictions using known information.)

4. Tell the student he or she will be reading the first half aloud to you so you can hear his or her reading. Tell the student that he or she will read the rest of the selection silently.

5. Start the timer when the student is ready. As the student reads, mark the exact phrases (or words) read using the following notations:

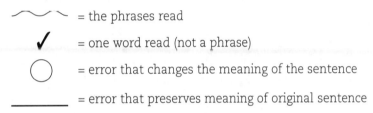

$\smile$ = the phrases read

✓ = one word read (not a phrase)

◯ = error that changes the meaning of the sentence

_____ = error that preserves meaning of original sentence

6. Stop the timer when the student reaches the end of the oral reading paragraph. Record this amount of time. Tell the student to continue reading silently. Start the timer. When the student is finished, stop the timer, and record this silent reading time.

7. Ask the student to tell you everything he or she remembered.

8. As the student retells the information recalled, you will be numbering the blanks in the retelling section to reflect the order in which the information was recalled. The numbers (versus check marks) are important because they will tell you the student's sequential recall level.

- Watch to see if the student first tells you something that he or she had as incorrect background knowledge. That is evidence of a student who did not read to learn.
- Watch for the student who recalls the last bit of information first and then goes backward. That indicates a powerful recency effect for that child.
- Watch for the student who only cites unrelated details without combining them into main ideas.

9. Ask the student the comprehension questions. Record the student's responses.

10. Calculate the words per minute. The circled number at the end of each reading selection indicates the number of words in that selection.

- Calculate Words Read Correctly: # of words read _____ – errors = words read correctly
- Calculate Words per Minute (WPM): # of words read correctly ____ x 60 ÷ # seconds to read the passage = _____ (WPM)

11. Send the student back to his or her activities and immediately analyze the information. This will help you target exactly what that student needs first.

Analyzing the Information You Recorded

1. Look at the student's background knowledge and his or her sequenced retelling.
- Did the student correct a misconception? If so, the student made connections between the print and previous assumptions.
- Did the student have limited background knowledge? Analyze how that related to responses. In the middle grades, students should be able to read and learn with limited prior knowledge.

2. Look at the student's prediction.
- Did the student restate the title as a prediction? If so, the student does not use known information to form predictions; a mini-lesson will be necessary.
- Did the student tie in other background knowledge? If so, the student is ready to learn from text.

3. Look at the number of decoding errors you marked. What do they have in common?
- Did the student read words incorrectly and keep going? If so, then no meaning was used, and the student needs a mini-lesson on how to monitor his or her comprehension.
- Did the student struggle with multisyllabic words? If so, the student needs help with breaking words into chunks.

4. Look at the phrased chunks you marked.
- Did the student read word by word (mostly check marks) or in phrases? If the student read word by word, then he or she requires individual direct fluency instruction. If the phrased chunks are consistently less than four-word phrases, then the activities in this book should be used in small groups or individualized based on the length of the phrases and the level of comprehension.

5. Look at the length of time it took the student to read orally and silently. Which is faster? Now go straight to the retelling.
- Did the student retell more information orally or silently? If you see a discrepancy, then you have identified a student who comprehends better at this point either orally or silently. (Usually, the difference shows that the student has higher oral comprehension than silent. This student needs to be able to do all independent reading while reading aloud in a whisper voice.)

6. Look at the retelling. The ability to retell without prompts is a higher level of comprehension than answering questions that aid recall.
- Did the student retell in order? This student has a good sequential memory.
- Did the student retell backward? The recency effect was in place.
- Did the student bounce around with details? If so, the student needs a mini-lesson on recalling information in sequence.
- Did the student retell only what was read orally? This student does not comprehend well when reading silently. All classroom reading should involve reading aloud for that student.
- Did the student retell the numerical information first? This indicates a good visual memory.

7. Look at the comprehension questions.
- Did the student recall only explicit information? This student is literal in reading and needs a mini-lesson on making connections to text, elaborations, and inferences—thinking beyond the reading.
- Did the student miss most of the questions? Look at the phrasing ability. Often, this student is suffering from a lack of fluency.

The Man Behind the Mobile

Alexander Calder was the son of a sculptor and a painter. His family moved often and Calder was encouraged by his parents to create toys and artwork out of found objects. His first creations were a duck and a dog cut from a sheet of copper. The duck rocked back and forth when you tapped it.

He had an early interest in the circus and his first major artwork was a tiny circus made from wire, leather, and cloth. It included tiny performers and animals. The artwork was a performance piece. Calder would move each piece to walk the audience through the two-hour circus performance.

Calder began to create large sculptures entirely from wire. They looked a bit like three-dimensional line drawings. From there, he added other elements, like paper and metal shapes. They often moved in the wind. Another artist from the time told him he should call the moving sculptures mobiles, and an entirely new art form was born. His sculptures that did not move were called stabiles. The terms mobiles and stabiles are still commonly used in art today.

Sea Turtles

Sea turtles are reptiles. They have scales and a backbone, and they breathe with lungs. They are cold-blooded animals, so their body temperature changes when their environment changes.

Sea turtles hatch from eggs, become hatchlings, and then grow into adults. The females return to the beach on which they were born every two to three years. They lay their eggs there. We do not know how they find their way back to the place of their birth.

Sea turtles are different from freshwater turtles in many ways. For example, sea turtles cannot pull their bodies into their shells for protection. Sea turtles only come ashore to lay their eggs. Other turtles can be found on land and in water. Sea turtles have excellent hearing and vision that allows them to exist in their dark environment. Freshwater turtles cannot see or hear well at all. Finally, while it is common knowledge that turtles move slowly on land, sea turtles use their flippers and streamlined bodies to swim long distances at fast speeds. These differences continue to fascinate those who love these endangered species.

Michael Faraday

Michael Faraday was an English scientist. He invented the first electric generator in 1831. Power plants around the world now use generators that are based on his invention. Faraday may be one of the greatest practical scientists of the 1800s. He made important discoveries in chemistry and physics.

Faraday's father was often ill and unable to work. Faraday was unable to attend school because he had to help support his siblings. Instead, he learned to read and write in Sunday school. When he was a teen he worked for a bookbinder. He often read the books there. He soon developed an interest in the science books.

He began to make his own simple experiments in electricity. He had to create all of his own scientific equipment. He took careful notes of his work. Eventually, he persuaded a well-known chemist to employ him as an assistant. He was soon considered a respectable chemist as well.

Late in his life, Queen Victoria recognized Faraday for his contributions. He declined an offer of knight-hood, but he did accept a retirement home given in appreciation.

Water Dragons

Walk into any pet store in America and you will find an odd assortment of tiny creatures to take home as a family pet. Among the goldfish, hamsters, and parakeets, you may also find leopard geckos, tree frogs, corn snakes, and water dragons. Looking like a small, slender iguana, the water dragon is far more active and curious than many of the other creatures in the reptile section. As you stand and stare, it may tilt its head and stare back.

The water dragon's body is only one-third its total length. Most of the lizard is its tail. Like many reptiles, it hatches from an egg, sheds its skin regularly as it grows, eats insects and small mammals for food, and needs sunlight to warm up and shady spots to cool down. Like a chameleon, the water dragon changes from green to brown and back again to match its surroundings. It may also turn brown when it is unhappy and green when it is pleased.

Water dragons are sometimes called Chinese water dragons, but they are imported to America from Vietnam, Cambodia, Thailand, and southern China. They are arboreal, or tree dwelling, lizards that choose trees with branches that hang over the water. When a predator threatens the lizards, they drop off the branch and into the water to swim away. They often head for shore after a short period. Once on land, they scurry away in a nearly upright position, running on their two back legs. Their strong tail presses against the ground to steady them.

Developing Reading Fluency • Gr. 6–8 © 2004 Creative Teaching Press

Name _____ Date _____

The Man Behind the Mobile

Background Questions

What is a mobile? _____ known/unknown

How do you think the mobile got its name? _____ known/unknown

Who invented the mobile? _____ known/unknown

What else do you know about the inventor of the mobile? _____ known/unknown

Prediction

What do you think you will learn when you read this selection called *The Man Behind the Mobile?*

_____

_____

Decoding and Fluency

Alexander Calder was the son of a sculptor and a painter. His family moved often and Calder was encouraged by his parents to create toys and artwork out of found objects. His first creations were a duck and a dog cut from a sheet of copper. The duck rocked back and forth when you tapped it.

He had an early interest in the circus and his first major artwork was a tiny circus made from wire, leather, and cloth. It included tiny performers and animals. The artwork was a performance piece. Calder would move each piece to walk the audience through the two-hour circus performance.

 105 | **Oral reading time:** | | errors | | **meaning-changing errors**

Calder began to create large sculptures entirely from wire. They looked a bit like three-dimensional line drawings. From there, he added other elements, like paper and metal shapes. They often moved in the wind. Another artist from the time told him he should call the moving sculptures mobiles, and an entirely new art form was born. His sculptures that did not move were called stabiles. The terms mobiles and sta-biles are still commonly used in art today.

 77 | **Silent reading time:** |

Developing Reading Fluency • Gr. 6–8 © 2004 Creative Teaching Press

Name _____   Date _____

Scoring Form

<table>
<tr><td colspan="2">

Reading Rate

ORAL   SILENT

WPM = _____   WPM = _____

Expression: yes   no

Read punctuation: yes   no
</td><td>

Phrasing
(look at swoops and check marks)

_____ word by word
_____ some words and some 2-word phrases
_____ mostly 2-word phrases
_____ 2- and 3-word phrases
_____ 3- and 4-word phrases
_____ phrases of 4 or more words consistently
</td></tr>
</table>

Retelling: "Tell me everything you read and learned about the man behind the mobile."

ORAL	SILENT
_____ Alexander Calder	_____ entirely from wire
_____ son of a sculptor	_____ looked like 3-D line drawings
_____ and a painter	_____ added elements like paper and metal shapes
_____ family moved often	_____ often moved in the wind
_____ was encouraged to create toys and artwork	_____ another artist named moving sculptures
_____ out of found objects	mobiles
_____ first creations were duck and dog	_____ birth of new art form
_____ cut from a sheet of copper	_____ stabiles were sculptures that did not move
_____ duck rocked when tapped	_____ terms mobiles and stabiles are still used in art
_____ had interest in circus	
_____ first major artwork was tiny circus	
_____ from wire, leather, and cloth	
_____ included tiny performers and animals	
_____ was a performance piece	
_____ would move each piece	
_____ through two-hour circus performance	

Discrepancy between oral and silent?   yes   no   (circle one)

Sequenced?   beg. to end   end to beg.   random   (circle one)

Comprehension questions: (Look for questions already answered in retelling.)

Explicit (in the text)

_____ **1.** Describe Calder's first two pieces of art. **ORAL** (duck and dog cut from copper sheet)

_____ **2.** What was his first major artwork? **ORAL** (a tiny circus)

_____ **3.** What is a mobile? **SILENT** (a sculpture that moves)

_____ **4.** What is a stabile? **SILENT** (a sculpture that does not move)

Implicit (inferences, elaborations, making connections)

_____ **5.** How do you think his childhood affected his art? (moving toys and art closely connected)

_____ **6.** What are some examples of found objects? (wire, leather, cloth, driftwood)

_____ **7.** Why are mobiles popular? (movement makes them interesting)

_____ **8.** Does the word *sculpture* more commonly refer to a mobile or a stabile? (stabile)

8 = independent   **6 or 7 = instructional**   **5 or less = too challenging**   **Total _____**

Developing Reading Fluency • Gr. 6–8 © 2004 Creative Teaching Press

Name _____   Date _____

Sea Turtles

Background Questions

What animals are related to sea turtles? _____ known/unknown

Where are sea turtles born? _____ known/unknown

What do you know about cold-blooded animals? _____ known/unknown

What do you know about sea turtles? _____ known/unknown

Prediction

What do you think you will learn when you read this selection called *Sea Turtles?*

_____

_____

Decoding and Fluency

Sea turtles are reptiles. They have scales and a backbone, and they breathe with lungs. They are cold-blooded animals, so their body temperature changes when their environment changes.

Sea turtles hatch from eggs, become hatchlings, and then grow into adults. The females return to the beach on which they were born every two to three years. They lay their eggs there. We do not know how they find their way back to the place of their birth.

 Oral reading time: ⬜ **errors** ⬜ **meaning-changing errors**

Sea turtles are different from freshwater turtles in many ways. For example, sea turtles cannot pull their bodies into their shells for protection. Sea turtles only come ashore to lay their eggs. Other turtles can be found on land and in water. Sea turtles have excellent hearing and vision that allows them to exist in their dark environment. Freshwater turtles cannot see or hear well at all. Finally, while it is common knowledge that turtles move slowly on land, sea turtles use their flippers and streamlined bodies to swim long distances at fast speeds. These differences continue to fascinate those who love these endangered species.

 Silent reading time:

Developing Reading Fluency • Gr. 6–8 © 2004 Creative Teaching Press

Informal Reading Inventories

Name _____   Date _____

Scoring Form

<table>
<tr><td>

Reading Rate

ORAL	SILENT
WPM = _____	WPM = _____
Expression:	yes	no
Read punctuation:	yes	no

</td><td>

Phrasing
(look at swoops and check marks)

_____ word by word
_____ some words and some 2-word phrases
_____ mostly 2-word phrases
_____ 2- and 3-word phrases
_____ 3- and 4-word phrases
_____ phrases of 4 or more words consistently

</td></tr>
</table>

Retelling: "Tell me everything you read and learned about *sea turtles*."

<table>
<tr><td>

ORAL

_____ sea turtles are reptiles
_____ scales, backbone, breathe with lungs
_____ cold-blooded animals
_____ so body temperature changes when environment
     changes
_____ hatch from eggs
_____ become hatchlings
_____ grow into adults
_____ females return to beach
_____ where they were born
_____ every two to three years
_____ lay their eggs there
_____ do not know how they find their way

</td><td>

SILENT

_____ sea turtles different from freshwater turtles
_____ sea turtles cannot pull bodies into shells for
     protection
_____ sea turtles come ashore only to lay eggs
_____ other turtles found on land and in water
_____ sea turtles have excellent hearing and vision
_____ allows dark environment
_____ freshwater turtles cannot see or hear well
_____ turtles move slowly on land
_____ sea turtles use flippers and streamlined bodies
     to swim long distances
_____ at fast speeds
_____ endangered species

</td></tr>
</table>

Discrepancy between oral and silent?	**yes**	**no**	(circle one)
Sequenced?	**beg. to end**	**end to beg.** **random**	(circle one)

Comprehension questions: (Look for questions already answered in retelling.)

Explicit (in the text)

_____ **1.** Name two characteristics of reptiles. **ORAL** (scales, backbone, lungs, cold-blooded)
_____ **2.** Why do female sea turtles return to their birth beach? **ORAL** (to lay eggs)
_____ **3.** What are some advantages that sea turtles have over freshwater turtles? **SILENT** (better sight
     and hearing)
_____ **4.** What helps sea turtles swim quickly? **SILENT** (flippers and streamlined bodies)

Implicit (inferences, elaborations, making connections)

_____ **5.** What does it mean to be an endangered species? (protected by law, but not many living)
_____ **6.** How might burying the eggs in sand help them? (sand keeps them warm, protected)
_____ **7.** You find a turtle at the park. Is it most likely a freshwater or sea turtle? Why? (freshwater, because sea
     turtles only come ashore to bury their eggs in the sand at the beach)
_____ **8.** How might a sea turtle protect itself? (swim quickly away)

8 = independent   **6 or 7 = instructional**   **5 or less = too challenging**   **Total** _____

Developing Reading Fluency • Gr. 6–8 © 2004 Creative Teaching Press

Name _____   Date _____

Michael Faraday

Background Questions

Who is Michael Faraday? _____ known/unknown

What does a bookbinder do? _____ known/unknown

How did Faraday come to study chemistry? _____ known/unknown

What else do you know about Michael Faraday? _____ known/unknown

Prediction

What do you think you will learn when you read this selection called *Michael Faraday?*

_____

_____

Decoding and Fluency

Michael Faraday was an English scientist. He invented the first electric generator in 1831. Power plants around the world now use generators that are based on his invention. Faraday may be one of the greatest practical scientists of the 1800s. He made important discoveries in chemistry and physics.

Faraday's father was often ill and unable to work. Faraday was unable to attend school because he had to help support his siblings. Instead, he learned to read and write in Sunday school. When he was a teen he worked for a bookbinder. He often read the books there. He soon developed an interest in the science books.

(106) | **Oral reading time:** | | **errors** | | **meaning-changing errors**

He began to make his own simple experiments in electricity. He had to create all of his own scientific equipment. He took careful notes of his work. Eventually, he persuaded a well-known chemist to employ him as an assistant. He was soon considered a respectable chemist as well.

Late in his life, Queen Victoria recognized Faraday for his contributions. He declined an offer of knighthood, but he did accept a retirement home given in appreciation.

(74) | **Silent reading time:**

Developing Reading Fluency • Gr. 6–8 © 2004 Creative Teaching Press

Informal Reading Inventories

Name _____   Date _____

Scoring Form

Reading Rate				Phrasing

Reading Rate

ORAL   SILENT

WPM = _____   WPM = _____

Expression: yes   no

Read punctuation: yes   no

Phrasing

(look at swoops and check marks)

_____ word by word

_____ some words and some 2-word phrases

_____ mostly 2-word phrases

_____ 2- and 3-word phrases

_____ 3- and 4-word phrases

_____ phrases of 4 or more words consistently

Retelling: "Tell me everything you read and learned about Michael Faraday."

ORAL

_____ Michael Faraday was an English scientist

_____ invented first electric generator in 1831

_____ power plants use generators based on his invention

_____ Faraday a great practical scientist of the 1800s

_____ made important discoveries in chemistry and physics

_____ Faraday's father often ill

_____ unable to work

_____ Faraday unable to attend school

_____ had to help support his siblings

_____ learned to read and write in Sunday school

_____ as a teen he worked for a bookbinder

_____ often read the books there

_____ developed an interest in the science books

SILENT

_____ began to do simple experiments

_____ in electricity

_____ had to create own scientific equipment

_____ took careful notes of his work

_____ persuaded a well-known chemist

_____ to employ him as an assistant

_____ soon considered a respectable chemist as well

_____ late in his life

_____ Queen Victoria recognized Faraday

_____ for his contributions

_____ declined knighthood

_____ did accept retirement home

Discrepancy between oral and silent?   yes   no   (circle one)

Sequenced?   beg. to end   end to beg.   random   (circle one)

Comprehension questions: (Look for questions already answered in retelling.)

Explicit (in the text)

_____ **1.** What areas of science did Faraday impact? **ORAL** (chemistry, physics)

_____ **2.** How did Faraday start reading science books? **ORAL** (he worked for a bookbinder)

_____ **3.** What is unusual about Faraday's equipment? **SILENT** (he had to make it all himself)

_____ **4.** How did he record his experiments? **SILENT** (he took careful notes)

Implicit (inferences, elaborations, making connections)

_____ **5.** How might his notes have helped him get a job with the chemist? (they were well written)

_____ **6.** How did supporting his siblings help prepare him for life as a scientist? (worked long, hard hours)

_____ **7.** Why might he have declined the knighthood? (various answers)

_____ **8.** Why is Faraday important to us today? (invented the electrical generator)

8 = independent   6 or 7 = instructional   5 or less = too challenging   **Total** _____

Developing Reading Fluency • Gr. 6–8 © 2004 Creative Teaching Press

Name _____   Date _____

Water Dragons

Background Questions

What is a water dragon? _____ known/unknown

Where are water dragons from? _____ known/unknown

Where can you get one in the United States? _____ known/unknown

What else do you know about water dragons? _____ known/unknown

Prediction

What do you think you will learn when you read this selection called *Water Dragons*?

_____

_____

Decoding and Fluency

Walk into any pet store in America and you will find an odd assortment of tiny creatures to take home as a family pet. Among the goldfish, hamsters, and parakeets, you may also find leopard geckos, tree frogs, corn snakes, and water dragons. Looking like a small, slender iguana, the water dragon is far more active and curious than many of the other creatures in the reptile section. As you stand and stare, it may tilt its head and stare back.

The water dragon's body is only one-third its total length. Most of the lizard is its tail. Like many reptiles, it hatches from an egg, sheds its skin regularly as it grows, eats insects and small mammals for food, and needs sunlight to warm up and shady spots to cool down. Like a chameleon, the water dragon changes from green to brown and back again to match its surroundings. It may also turn brown when it is unhappy and green when it is pleased.

(165) | **Oral reading time:** | | errors | | **meaning-changing errors**

Water dragons are sometimes called Chinese water dragons, but they are imported to America from Vietnam, Cambodia, Thailand, and southern China. They are arboreal, or tree dwelling, lizards that choose trees with branches that hang over the water. When a predator threatens the lizards, they drop off the branch and into the water to swim away. They often head for shore after a short period. Once on land, they scurry away in a nearly upright position, running on their two back legs. Their strong tail presses against the ground to steady them

(92) | **Silent reading time:**

Developing Reading Fluency • Gr. 6–8 © 2004 Creative Teaching Press

Informal Reading Inventories

Name _____   Date _____

Scoring Form

Reading Rate		Phrasing

Reading Rate

ORAL   SILENT

WPM = _____   WPM = _____

Expression: yes   no

Read punctuation: yes   no

Phrasing
(look at swoops and check marks)

_____ word by word
_____ some words and some 2-word phrases
_____ mostly 2-word phrases
_____ 2- and 3-word phrases
_____ 3- and 4-word phrases
_____ phrases of 4 or more words consistently

Retelling: "Tell me everything you read and learned about water dragons."

ORAL

_____ in pet store
_____ find tiny creatures for pets
_____ geckos, frogs, snakes, and water dragons
_____ look like a small, slender iguana
_____ more active and curious than many other creatures in reptile section
_____ it may tilt its head and stare back
_____ body is only one-third its total length
_____ most of lizard is its tail
_____ hatches from an egg
_____ sheds skin regularly as it grows
_____ eats insects and small mammals
_____ needs sunlight to warm up
_____ shady spots to cool down
_____ like a chameleon
_____ green to brown and back again
_____ to match its surroundings
_____ brown when unhappy
_____ green when pleased

SILENT

_____ water dragons sometimes called Chinese water dragons
_____ imported to America from Vietnam, Cambodia, Thailand, and southern China
_____ arboreal, or tree dwelling, lizards
_____ choose trees with branches that hang over the water
_____ when predator threatens lizards
_____ they drop off the branch
_____ and into the water to swim away
_____ head for shore after a short period
_____ once on land, scurry away
_____ in nearly upright position
_____ running on two back legs
_____ strong tail presses against the ground to steady them

Discrepancy between oral and silent?	yes	no	(circle one)
Sequenced?	beg. to end	end to beg. random	(circle one)

Comprehension questions: (Look for questions already answered in retelling.)

Explicit (in the text)

_____ **1.** What do water dragons eat? **ORAL** (insects and small mammals)
_____ **2.** What can a water dragon change? **ORAL** (its color)
_____ **3.** What is an arboreal lizard? **SILENT** (one that lives in the trees)
_____ **4.** How does it escape a predator? **SILENT** (jumps in water and swims away)

Implicit (inferences, elaborations, making connections)

_____ **5.** How is a water dragon like a chameleon? (they both change colors for camouflage)
_____ **6.** Why might you keep a bucket of water for a captive water dragon? (they swim in water)
_____ **7.** What might be an advantage to being an active lizard? (can escape predators quickly)
_____ **8.** Leopard geckos, tree frogs, corn snakes, and water dragons are all a kind of _____. (reptile)

8 = independent   **6 or 7 = instructional**   **5 or less = too challenging**   **Total _____**

Developing Reading Fluency • Gr. 6–8 © 2004 Creative Teaching Press

Read-Arounds

According to research, one reason why students do not read with phrasing and fluency is that they do not have a solid base of high-frequency words and sight words, which is required for reading books independently. Research recommends activities that give students practice with frequently used words. This will in turn help with phrasing and fluency because students will not need to slow down to decode as often. The Read-Around cards in this section are already written in phrases (spaces between groups of words), so students can see and better understand how to read words in groups. The Read-Around cards are designed for groups of two to four students. This allows for optimal amounts of practice and active involvement. The phrases on the cards are short and simple to help students focus directly on reading phrases and practicing high-frequency and content words.

Strategies: phrased reading; repeated oral reading; active listening; reading high-frequency, content, and sight words

Materials
- construction paper or tagboard
- envelopes
- scissors

Directions

1. Choose a set of cards (e.g., figurative language, propaganda), and copy the cards on construction paper or tagboard. (Each set of cards is two pages.) Cut apart the cards, and laminate them so that they can be reused throughout the school year. Put the cards in an envelope, and write the title (e.g., *National Symbols*) on the envelope.

2. Give a set of cards to a small group of students so that each student has three to six cards. Review with students the pronunciation and meaning of the bold words and phrases on their clue cards so that they are familiar and comfortable with them (or preteach the words).

3. Explain that students will play a listening and reading game. Model how the game works and share the correct answers with each group the first time students play using a new set of cards. Read aloud each student's cards, and then have students silently read their cards at least five times to build fluency. Discuss each question and corresponding answer so students can concentrate more on reading fluently than on determining the answer to the question as they play.

4. Tell the group that the student who has the clue card that says *I have the first card* will begin the game by reading aloud his or her card. Then, have the student with the answer to the clue read aloud his or he card. Tell students to continue until they get back to the first card. (The game ends after a student reads *Who has the first card?* and a student answers *I have the first card.*)

5. Encourage students to play the game at least twice. Have students shuffle and deal the cards again so that students read different cards each time.

Extension

Invite students to take home a set of cards. Have them teach their families how to play and practice reading the cards with family members. Encourage families to make additional cards.

Making Inferences

I have the first card.
Kimberly wants a pet. She is allergic to cats. Her mom is scared of mice.
Her dad doesn't want to buy crickets for a reptile. What pet might she get?

She might get a dog, since she can't have a reptile or a cat.
In his free time, Joey draws pictures of animals. He has journals at home
in which he doodles. What might he have when he grows up?

He might have an art gallery full of his own artwork.
Keith earns $15.00 a week in allowance every Friday. By Monday of every
week, he is broke. What can you assume about Keith?

He is not in the habit of saving money.
For his birthday, Dave made a list of what he hoped to receive
as gifts. The list included a new stereo, a portable DVD player,
a new bike, and a trip to Hawaii. What might you conclude about Dave?

He is used to getting **extravagant** gifts.
Ashley organized and held a bake sale. She gave all of the money
to her local animal shelter. She did this every month.
What can you assume about Ashley?

She is kind and generous and has a passion for helping animals.
A commercial shows strong, good-looking people drinking a vitamin drink
called Triple Power. What do the advertisers want you to think?

You will be strong and good looking if you drink their **product.**
Mr. James didn't know his child got a detention. Mr. James didn't fill out
the registration forms for his child to go on the field trip. Mr. James
doesn't share books with his child. What might be true of Mr. James?

He might not be able to read.
Spotty eats carrots. He lives in a cage. He's scared of cats.
and most other animals. What might you assume about Spotty?

Developing Reading Fluency • Gr 6–8 © 2004 Creative Teaching Press

Making Inferences

He's a rabbit.
Linda has never   been in a pool,   although she's over forty years old.
She has never been   on a boat.   She lives on a farm   in West Virginia.
What might you assume   about Linda?

She cannot swim.
Arthur loves to play basketball   with his family.   In his free time,   he enjoys wood-
working   and tending a vegetable garden.   What might you assume   about Arthur?

He likes to work with his hands.
Kimberly does not eat granola.   She would be rushed to the school nurse
if she had   chocolate chip peanut butter ice cream   at a school party.
What might you assume   about Kimberly?

She is allergic to peanuts.
Danielle has a backpack   with a ticket,   a luggage claim ticket,   a book,
and headphones. She had to turn   her cell phone off.   Where might she be?

She might be on an airplane.
Mark brings his dog everywhere,   even if there is a sign   that says No Dogs
Allowed.   Mark pays close attention   to the sounds around him.
What might you believe about Mark?

He is blind.
On his way to work,   Anthony packed his shovel,   a rake,
and trash bags.   What might you conclude   Anthony does for a living?

He might be a gardener.
Robert sees patterns   everywhere he goes.   He likes to count
by sevens and eights   on long car trips.
His mother makes up word problems   for him to solve in the car.
What might you assume about Robert?

He might be   a mathematician someday.
Who has the first card?

Developing Reading Fluency • Gr. 6–8 © 2004 Creative Teaching Press

Propaganda and Persuasion Techniques

I have the first card.
What do you call   what we often see   in advertisements,   commercials,   and newspapers that doesn't always   tell the truth   and sometimes stretches the truth?

I have the use   of propaganda.
Who has the purpose   of propaganda?

I have the goal   of influencing someone's opinion   for personal gain.
Who has the technique   used in propaganda   that tries to convince you   that you'll be left out   if you don't do   what they do?   In other words,   everyone is doing it   so you should, too!

I have   the bandwagon technique.   Hop on   the bandwagon!
Who has the technique   used in propaganda   that makes something bad sound much better   by using different words?

I have   the technique of using euphemisms   (passed away   —not died).
Who has the technique used in propaganda   that plays on your emotions and scares you   into doing something?

I have   the technique of using fear   to prompt action.
Who has the technique used in propaganda   that tries to attach   a negative label or name   to an opponent?

I have   the technique of name-calling.
Who has the technique used in propaganda   by politicians and advertisers   to make you think   they are just like you—   just ordinary citizens?

I have   the plain folks technique.
Who has the technique used in propaganda   that uses personal experience   to convince you   to buy a product?   For example,   an athlete   talks about how certain shoes   helped him play better   in the last game.

Developing Reading Fluency • Gr. 6–8 © 2004 Creative Teaching Press

Propaganda and Persuasion Techniques

I have the technique of using testimonials. Who has the technique used in propaganda that tries to carry over the approval or disapproval of a valued person to a product? For example, if the president likes Fruity Os Cereal, then it is good for America.

I have the transfer technique. Who has the propaganda technique used by politicians and advertisers to make themselves look friendly and funny?

I have the humor technique. Who has the technique used in propaganda by politicians and famous people to make themselves look good in bad situations by giving a prepared speech to a television crew?

I have the use of a press conference. Who has the technique most commonly used today in TV shows and movies that shows stars using particular brands of products or those products in the background of the show to make viewers want the product just like the stars have?

I have the technique of product placement. Who has the propaganda technique of saying or showing something over and over again until people actually begin to believe it?

I have the technique of repetition. Who has the propaganda technique that often involves e-mail rumors, or gossip?

I have the word of mouth technique. Who has the propaganda technique that involves a person, company, or business writing an article for the newspaper to make itself look good?

I have the technique of planting a press article. Who has the first card?

Developing Reading Fluency • Gr. 6–8 © 2004 Creative Teaching Press

Fun with Figurative Language and Poetry

I have the first card.
Who has the name   of the type of figurative language   demonstrated in this statement: He had tons   of money!

That was an example   of hyperbole   since it was a big exaggeration.
Who has the name   of the type of figurative language   demonstrated in this statement: He was a songbird.

That was an example   of a metaphor   since it represented him   but really wasn't what he was.   Who has the name   of the type of figurative language   demonstrated in this statement: She was as graceful   as a swan.

That was an example   of a simile   since it compared her   to something else.
Who has the name   of the type of figurative language   demonstrated in this statement: Five friendly frogs   fainted feverishly.

That was an example   of alliteration   since each word began   with the same sound.
Who has the name   of the type of figurative language   demonstrated in this statement: He was clearly confused.

That was an example   of an oxymoron   since two words   have opposite meanings.
Who has the name   of the type of figurative language   demonstrated in this statement: No pain, no gain.

That was an example   of a cliché   since the phrase has become so common.
Who has the name   of the type of figurative language   demonstrated in this statement: She sings   at the top of her lungs.

That was an example   of an idiom   since the phrase can not be translated literally.
Who has the name   of the type of figurative language   demonstrated in this statement: The little puppy smiled   as the young girl hugged him   tightly.

Developing Reading Fluency • Gr. 6–8 © 2004 Creative Teaching Press

Fun with Figurative Language and Poetry

That was an example   of personification since the subject had human qualities.
Who has the name   of a long, narrative poem   that usually involves   the actions
of a heroic figure?

I have the epic poem.
Who has the name   of a short,   narrative poem   that was written to be sung?

I have the ballad.
Who has the name   of the funny five-line poem   told in verse   in which   the
first, second, and fifth lines   rhyme   and the third and fourth lines   rhyme?

I have the limerick.
Who has the name   of a type of poetry   that does not rhyme   or have a rhythm?

I have free verse.
Who has the name   of a type of poetry   that does not rhyme   but is formed   by
the first letters   of a particular word?

I have the acrostic poem.
Who has the name   of the brief type of poetry   that has a maximum   of
17 syllables ?

I have the haiku poem.
Who has the name   of the type of poem   that uses specific parts of speech   for each
word   in a particular format?

I have the diamonte poem.
Who has the first card?

Developing Reading Fluency • Gr. 6-8 © 2004 Creative Teaching Press

National Symbols

I have the first card.
What does the color red represent   in the stripes   of our flag?

That color represents courage.
What does the color white represent   in the stripes   of our flag?

That color represents liberty.
What does the color blue represent   in the field   of our flag?

That color represents justice.
Which national symbol do you think of   when you hear these clues: rings,
cracked copper,   and Philadelphia?

That reminds me   of the national symbol   of the Liberty Bell.
Which animal   is the Republican Party's mascot?

It is the elephant.
Which animal   is the Democratic Party's mascot?

It is the donkey.
What image do you picture   when you envision   an olive branch,   arrows,
and a bald eagle?

That reminds me   of the Great Seal.
What image do you picture   when you think of   a striped costume,
the army,   and Sam Wilson?

Developing Reading Fluency • Gr. 6–8 © 2004 Creative Teaching Press

National Symbols

That reminds me   of Uncle Sam.
What image do you picture   when you envision   immigrants,   the country
of France,   and freedom?

That reminds me   of the Statue of Liberty.
What image do you picture   when you envision   Pilgrims,   a ship,
and Plymouth Rock?

That reminds me   of the Mayflower.
What comes to mind   when you think about   what laws are based upon,
the powers of the branches of government,   and the framework of our government?

That reminds me   of the Constitution.
What image do you picture   when you hear: talons, powerful,
and an endangered species?

That reminds me   of the bald eagle.
What image do you picture   when you hear: four presidents,   mountain carving,
and the Black Hills   of South Dakota?

That reminds me   of Mount Rushmore.
What image do you picture   when you hear: Oval Office,
first home to John Adams,   frequently toured?

That reminds me   of the White House.
What image do you picture   when you hear: white marble,
tribute to a president,   and his speech   of the Gettysburg Address?

That reminds me   of the Lincoln Memorial.
Who has the first card?

Developing Reading Fluency • Gr. 6–8 © 2004 Creative Teaching Press

Read-Arounds

Famous Historical Figures

I have the first card.
Who has the name of the author of the Declaration of Independence?

I have President Thomas Jefferson.
Who has the name of the person who helped Captain John Smith and the Jamestown colonists?

I have the important historical figure Pocahontas.
Who has the name of the man who won the Battle of Yorktown in 1781?

I have General and President George Washington.
Who has the name of the man who was killed at the Boston Massacre in the year 1770?

I have Crispus Attucks.
Who has the name of the man who led the Civil Rights Movement?

I have the famous orator Martin Luther King, Jr.
Who has the name of the man who led the nation through the Civil War and now has a marble memorial in Washington, D.C.?

I have President Abraham Lincoln.
Who has the name of the man who invented the first practical electric light bulb?

I have Thomas Edison.
Who has the name of the first American woman to travel into space?

Developing Reading Fluency • Gr. 6–8 © 2004 Creative Teaching Press

Famous Historical Figures

I have Sally Ride.
Who has the name   of the guide and interpreter   for the famous Lewis and Clark?

I have Sacagawea.
Who has the name   of the author   of the American classic   titled Tom Sawyer?

I have Mark Twain.
Who has the name   of the president   who led the nation
through the Great Depression   and World War II?

I have President Franklin D. Roosevelt.
Who has the name   of the man who is credited   with the invention   of the telephone?

I have Alexander Graham Bell.
Who has the name   of the man famous   for the following quote:
Give me liberty,   or give me death!

I have Patrick Henry.
Who has the name   of the man famous   for the following quote: We must
indeed   all hang together, or most assuredly   we shall hang separately.

I have Benjamin Franklin.
Who has the name   of the woman   who was an escaped slave
and became famous   for leading the Underground Railroad?

I have Harriet Tubman.
Who has the first card?

Read-Arounds

Economics 101

I have the first card.
Who has the name   of the type of resources   that occur in nature
such as land,   rocks, water, iron, oil,   and coal?

I have natural resources.
Who has the name   of the type of resource   that includes the people
who do the labor   on a job?

I have human resources.
Who has the name   of the type of resources   that include things
made by people   such as factories,   machines,   and plows?

I have capital resources.
Who has the name   of the movement   of goods and services   between countries?

I have international trade.
Who has the word that describes   how goods and services   are produced in
one country   but sold and sent out   to another country?

I have what is exported.
Who has the word that describes   how goods and services   are produced in a foreign
country   but are bought   and brought into your country?

I have what is imported.
Who has the word that describes   what you are when you buy
goods or services   that you need or want?

Developing Reading Fluency • Gr. 6–8 © 2004 Creative Teaching Press

Economics 101

I have a consumer.
Who has the word that describes the business goal to make more money than is spent?

I have profit.
Who has the result of the circumstance when there is more demand for a product than there is a supply?

I have the result of the price going up.
Who has the word that describes the financial strategy that prevents spending more than you have?

I have a budget.
Who has the words that describe a safe place to save money for your future?

I have a savings account.
Who has the word that describes how people traded goods and services before money was created?

I have the barter system.
Who has the name of the method of creating products that involves many people working as a team, with each team member performing one part in the creation of the product?

I have an assembly line.
Who has the extra fees paid to the government when you buy goods or services and which pay for public services?

I have taxes.
Who has the first card?

Developing Reading Fluency • Gr. 6–8 © 2004 Creative Teaching Press

Square Roots and Exponents

I have the first card.
Who has the value of   the square root   of sixty-four?

I have eight.
Who has the value of   twelve squared?

I have one hundred forty-four.
Who has the value of   three raised to   the third power?

I have twenty-seven.
Who has the value of   the square root   of eighty-one?

I have nine.
Who has the value of   five raised to   the third power?

I have one hundred twenty-five.
Who has the value of   the square root   of one hundred twenty-one?

I have eleven.
Who has the value of   two raised to   the fifth power?

I have thirty-two.
Who has the value of   the square root   of twenty-five?

Developing Reading Fluency • Gr. 6–8 © 2004 Creative Teaching Press

Square Roots and Exponents

I have five.
Who has the value of   four squared?

I have sixteen.
Who has the value of   the square root   of one hundred?

I have ten.
Who has the value of   the square root   of forty-nine?

I have seven.
Who has the value of   one raised to   the tenth power?

I have one.
Who has the value of   ten raised to   the fifth power?

I have one hundred thousand.
Who has the value of   the square root   of four hundred?

I have twenty.
Who has the value of   the square root   of thirty-six?

I have six.
Who has the first card?

Read-Arounds

Roman Numerals

I have the first card.
Who has the value   of the roman numerals   XX?

I have that value.   Those roman numerals represent twenty.
Who has the value   of the roman numeral   L?

I have that value.   That roman numeral represents fifty.
Who has the value   of the roman numeral   M?

I have that value.   That roman numeral represents one thousand.
Who has the value   of the roman numerals   XIV?

I have that value.   Those roman numerals represent fourteen.
Who has the value   of the roman numerals   XVIII?

I have that value.   Those roman numerals represent eighteen.
Who has the value   of the roman numerals   XXXIV?

I have that value.   Those roman numerals represent thirty-four.
Who has the value   of the roman numerals   XXVII?

I have that value.   Those roman numerals represent twenty-seven.
Who has the value   of the roman numeral   D?

Developing Reading Fluency • Gr. 6-8 © 2004 Creative Teaching Press

Roman Numerals

I have that value.   Those roman numeral equal five hundred.
Who has the value   of the roman numerals   LVII?

I have that value.   Those roman numerals represent fifty-seven.
Who has the value   of the roman numerals   XLV?

I have that value.   Those roman numerals represent forty-five.
Who has the value   of the roman numerals   CV?

I have that value. Those roman numerals represent one hundred five.
Who has the value   of the roman numerals   CCXC?

I have that value.   Those roman numerals represent   two hundred ninety.
Who has the value   of the roman numerals   LIX?

I have that value.   Those roman numerals represent   fifty-nine.
Who has the value   of the roman numerals   XD?

I have that value.   Those roman numerals represent   four hundred ninety.
Who has the value   of the roman numerals   MMMM?

I have that value.   Those roman numerals represent   four thousand.
Who has the first card?

Developing Reading Fluency • Gr. 6-8 © 2004 Creative Teaching Press

Read-Arounds

Phrasing Fun

Students who are still not reading with phrasing and fluency will have a difficult time with the transition from learning to read to reading to learn. This skill is critical for middle-school success due to the link between phrasing and comprehension. If a student is still focusing on the decoding process of the text, then he or she is unable to focus on the meaning behind the words he or she is busy decoding. This impedes the comprehension process and breaks down learning. These students need many opportunities to listen to phrasing and practice reading phrased chunks of between three and five words. They must transfer this practice into ongoing text. The fun, motivating activities in this section put the emphasis on meaning rather than decoding. Each Phrasing Fun activity was designed for one-on-one guided instruction, small groups, or whole-class instruction on the overhead projector. By following the Fantastic Five Format, the student is assured success in meaningful phrasing practice to develop fluency and comprehension.

Strategies: phrased reading; repeated oral reading; active listening; reading high-frequency, content, and sight words

Materials
- no additional materials are required

Directions

1. Copy a class set or group set of each pair of Phrasing Fun stories.

2. Give each student a copy of the first page of the pair of reproducibles for the story you have chosen.

3. Read the text following the Fantastic Five Format (described on page 8).

> Step 1: Modeled Fluency—Model how to read each phrase.
> Step 2: Echo Reading—Read one phrase at a time as students repeat.
> Step 3: Choral Reading—Guide students as they read with phrasing along with you.
> Step 4: Independent Fluency—Have students read the phrases to you.
> Step 5: Reverse Echo Reading—Have students read the phrases, and then repeat their phrasing, expression, and fluency.

4. Give each student a copy of the second page of the reproducible for the story you have chosen. (It has the same phrases as reproducible 1, but it is written in an ongoing text format and has at least two additional paragraphs of related text. This reproducible gives students the opportunity to transfer their fluently read phrases to a paragraph format.)

5. Choral read the reproducible together. Then, invite the group to read it aloud to you.

6. Repeat this activity with additional reading selections for further practice.

7. Invite students to practice their phrasing and fluency by reading a familiar book.

Extension

Copy a page from a class textbook. Have students use a pencil to draw slash marks to break apart the first paragraph into phrases (as in the first page of each set of reproducibles). Provide time for them to practice the Fantastic Five Format prior to reading the paragraph, and then have them continue through the rest of the page.

Clicker Training

What do zoos,

marine parks,

and dog training schools

use to train elephants,

whales, baboons, and dogs?

They are using

a small metal tool

called a clicker

that makes a sound like a sharp

double snap!

This method of behavior training

is called clicker training.

Clicker Training

What do zoos, marine parks, and dog training schools use to train elephants, whales, baboons, and dogs? They are using a small metal tool called a clicker that make a sound like a sharp double snap! This method of behavior training is called clicker training.

A clicker helps the trainer "take a picture" of the behavior he or she wants the animal to repeat. The animal does the behavior, the trainer clicks, and then the trainer follows up the click with a reward—usually food. Behavioral psychologists, who first used this tool many years ago, call it a secondary reinforcer. Primary reinforcers are the rewards that animals work for, such as food, affection, or fetching a ball. A secondary reinforcer is a signal that goes with the reward.

So how do you use the clicker? You can try this trick with your dog at home. If you do not have a clicker, use your tongue on the roof of your mouth to make a sharp "click, click." First, help the dog notice and like the click. Sit in front of your dog with the clicker and some treats. Being careful to keep the clicker away from the dog's ear, click and give the dog a treat. Do this twenty to thirty times. If your dog already knows the sit command, have him or her sit, click as soon as the dog sits, and give him or her a treat. Your dog will catch on quickly.

To teach your dog a new trick, try this one. Hold a ball in front of your dog's nose. Click and give the dog a treat if he or she investigates it. Repeat that step many times. Just stop throughout the day and do it again. When your dog starts to touch the object often to get treats, start naming it just before the dog's nose touches it. Say "ball," click, and then give the dog a treat. Repeat all the previous steps with two or three other objects, such as a tie, a book, and a block. Then, put all the objects on the ground and ask for them by name. Whenever the dog touches the correct object, click and give him or her a treat! Before you know it, your dog will be paying close attention to the sounds associated with that object and you can soon amaze your friends with the dog's clever identification of the right object.

Developing Reading Fluency • Gr. 6–8 © 2004 Creative Teaching Press

Masks

Masks may be

carved from wood.

They may be

made from molded plastic,

papier-mâché,

or cloth.

They may be undecorated.

They may be heavily decorated

with precious metals,

jewels, feathers, and paint.

Phrasing Fun

Masks

Masks may be carved from wood. They may be made from molded plastic, papier-mâché, or cloth. They may be undecorated. They may be heavily decorated with precious metals, jewels, feathers, and paint.

Masks may have an artistic purpose. In many cultures, masks are an important part of the theater. In ancient Greece, Rome, and Japan, actors used masks in all performances. Masks may also have a practical purpose such as the mask a beekeeper wears to protect his face. Japanese soldiers in the 1700s and Italian soldiers in the 1500s also used masks for armor.

Masks play many roles in African history. Their most important role may be ceremonial. They are usually used with an accompanying costume. Masks are often used with a specific dance or music. To really understand the nature of the mask, it is helpful to see it with its costume and dance. African masks are made of wood, natural materials, man-made cloth, and/or animal skin. Common African masks include face, cap, helmet, shoulder, and body masks.

African maskettes are smaller and not worn on the face. Maskettes include passport masks. These identify the wearer to other tribes and are worn on the arm.

Many modern celebrations still include the use of masks, even in urban American settings. Halloween and Mardi Gras are two examples of celebrations where masks still play an important role. Masks continue to play a part in the arts. They also continue to be used in a practical manner such as for protection in a hockey game. When was the last time *you* wore a mask?

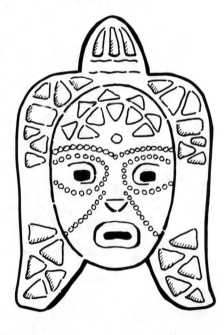 

Developing Reading Fluency • Gr. 6–8 © 2004 Creative Teaching Press

How Motorcycles Are Designed

Motorcycle manufacturers

create or design

the motorcycle of the future

in many ways.

One way is to go racing.

Companies create

exotic parts and new technology

and try the motorcycle on the racetrack.

If it wins races,

they refine the pieces

and sell them to the public.

Phrasing Fun

How Motorcycles Are Designed

Motorcycle manufacturers create or design the motorcycle of the future in many ways. One way is to go racing. Companies create exotic parts and new technology and try the motorcycle on the racetrack. If it wins races, they refine the pieces and sell them to the public.

For example, Doug Henry won a super cross race on a four-stroke motocross bike in 1997. At that time, almost all motocross bikes were two-strokes because they were lighter and more powerful than four-strokes. Since then four-stroke technology has progressed to the point where today the most popular motocross bikes sold are four-strokes.

Another way is through concept bikes. Companies do a lot of research, but they still don't know what the public wants to buy. They build wild bikes that take certain styling cues to extremes. They show them to the public and the media and listen to what people's reactions are. They use this information to plan the way the real bikes will look.

Many years ago, Honda showed a concept bike called the Zodia. There was very positive reaction from the public and the press. Today, styling cues and technology from the Zodia are found on the VTX, Honda's big cruiser motorcycle and also the Honda Rune, Honda's flagship cruiser. Both motorcycles sell very well.

In 2000, Honda showed a concept bike called the Xwing. People loved it so much that Honda styled the ST1300 after the bike. The resulting bike is not as extreme as the concept bike, but the two bikes are very similar.

Personal Jets!

In the movies,

a character straps

a jet pack on his or her back

and flies off to new adventures.

Could it happen in real life?

The answer is yes,

and no.

There are machines in development

that could take one person

off the ground

and into the air.

But they aren't as small

as a pack on the back

and they aren't jet propelled.

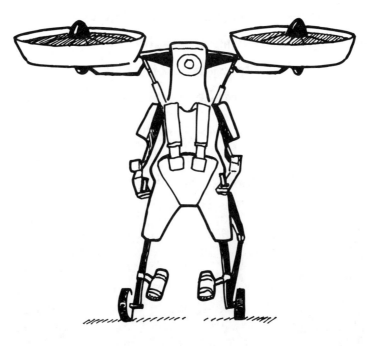

Phrasing Fun

Personal Jets!

In the movies, a character straps a jet pack on his or her back and flies off to new adventures. Could it happen in real life? The answer is yes, and no. There are machines in development that could take one person off the ground and into the air. But they aren't as small as a pack on the back and they aren't jet propelled.

The idea of a personal flyer is nothing new. Hiller Helicopters developed the first working crafts for one person during the 1940s and 1950s. The Hiller Flying Platform was developed during the mid-1950s using funds from the Office of Naval Research. A person could stand on a platform that was attached to a large rotating fan. It worked and a few prototypes were made for the military, but there were a number of problems with the design and in the end the idea was abandoned.

More recently, Trek Aerospace has developed the SoloTrek Exo-Skeletor Flying Vehicle (XFV). The craft first flew in December 2001, lifting a man a few feet off the ground. The machine is less like the jet pack of the movies and more like a combination of hovercraft and motorcycle.

The XFV used the same kind of ducted fan that the Hiller Flying Platform used, but the XFV uses two smaller fans. One fan is above the person's left shoulder and one is above his or her right shoulder. The XFV was controlled using two handgrips that allowed the user to change the speed and position of the fans individually. This made it possible for the craft to turn and spin, climb, and descend.

Today, the XFV has evolved into the Springtail EFV-4B. It works a lot like the XFV did, only better. It can fly up to 94 mph, go as high as a small aircraft, and is similar in size and weight to a motorcycle. It looks like a capital T, with the person standing on 2-foot pegs at the base of the T, and his or her head just below the cross of the T—the fans that lift the machine. Each fan has three blades that force the machine up. The engine is below the fans and behind the operator. A person operates the machine, but it features an advanced computer control system to work properly.

Can you buy one today? Well, no, the machine still needs a lot of research, work, and testing. Probably the first models will be used in the military, which is helping to pay for the development. However, it may only be a few years before you hear someone say, "I'm off to the store for milk! I think I'll take the EFV and skip the traffic!"

Developing Reading Fluency • Gr. 6–8 © 2004 Creative Teaching Press

Origami

Origami is

a folded paper sculpture.

The art of paper folding

was developed in Japan.

Long ago,

paper was folded in Japan

for ceremonial reasons.

Using special folds

helped discourage forgeries.

Then it was pursued

as a hobby.

It is the fun paper folding

that is the beginning

of modern origami.

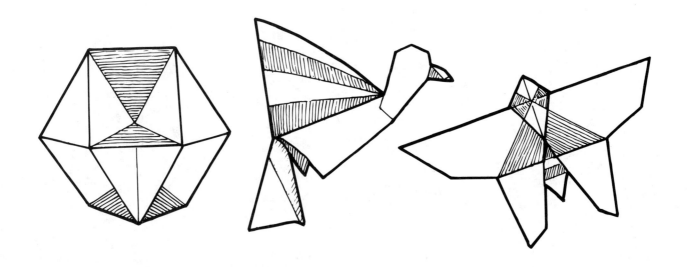

Phrasing Fun

Origami

Origami is a folded paper sculpture. The art of paper folding was developed in Japan. Long ago, paper was folded in Japan for ceremonial reasons. Using special folds helped discourage forgeries. Then it was pursued as a hobby. It is the fun paper folding that is the beginning of modern origami.

Origami patterns are called models. Some are quite simple. Others are very complex. Origami began in the early 1600s. It continued unchanged until the 1950s. Classic models include kimonos, boats, boxes, birds, and hats.

Originally, recycled paper was used. Eventually a strong, soft paper was developed. Today, origami paper has a blank side and a patterned side. Or, it may have different colors on each side. The contrast is part of the finished design.

Origami once included cutting the paper. Today, origami artists discourage this. A folded paper sculpture that includes cutting can be a work of art. Still, it is not considered true origami. However, origami may use more than one sheet of paper to make the model.

Akira Yoshizawa was the first modern Japanese origami artist. He introduced a variety of new models in 1952. He published photos of his new models in a magazine. These photos reawakened worldwide interest in the art. Other artists used his folds to make animals with four legs and a tail. Suddenly, the door was opened to a completely new world of origami!

Developing Reading Fluency • Gr. 6–8 © 2004 Creative Teaching Press

Phrased Text

Students who are not chunking groups of words in phrases end up with poorer comprehension since they are overly focusing on the print rather than the message hidden within. This explicit strategy is best for students who don't seem to understand the concept of chunking words. When most people speak, they phrase a whole sentence or thought as one phrase. Students have a hard time hearing the phrases, so telling them to "read like talking" doesn't always work. Some students simply require more explicit instruction. The activities in this section are designed for individuals, small groups, or even the whole class. They will provide the visual cues for those students struggling with understanding what a "phrase" really is.

Strategies: phrased reading; visual cues; apply and transfer; scaffolding phrase size

Materials
• no additional materials are required

Directions

1. Decide which students need practice with phrased text activities by using the assessments at the beginning of this book. Students who still read word-by-word or only two- to three-word phrases should participate.

2. Photocopy a set of phrased text reproducibles for each student.

3. Give each student a copy of the first page that contains the visual cue: ◆
Explain that he or she will train his or her eyes to look at chunks of words at a time. (Due to the explicit nature of the instruction, the student's mind will be focused on grouping words instead of on meaning. Therefore, rereading a few times for comprehension will be important.)

4. Read the first few sentences following the Fantastic Five Format (described on page 8).
> Step 1: Modeled Fluency—Model how to read each phrase.
> Step 2: Echo Reading—Read one phrase at a time as students repeat.
> Step 3: Choral Reading—Guide students as they read with phrasing along with you.
> Step 4: Independent Fluency—Have students read the phrases to you.
> Step 5: Reverse Echo Reading—Have students read the phrases, and then repeat their phrasing, expression, and fluency.

5. Have the student or group continue with the rest on its own.

6. Immediately read the page without visual cues together using the choral reading technique.

7. Finally, have students individually read the page without visual cues.

Extension

Invite students to preview the next section of a textbook or reading anthology you are using in class. Have them rewrite the paragraphs showing visual cues. Then, have them practice reading the phrased text before reading their textbook.

Popsicles! Popsicles!

What is better on a hot day ✦ than a cold Popsicle? ✦ The Popsicle was actually invented ✦ in the dead of winter ✦ in San Francisco, California! ✦ An eleven-year-old boy ✦ invented it.

On a cold, winter day ✦ in 1905, ✦ Frank Epperson was drinking punch ✦ on his porch. ✦ He liked to stir it ✦ with a drink stick. ✦ Then, ✦ Frank went into the house ✦ and left his punch outside. ✦ The next morning, ✦ Frank discovered that his punch ✦ had frozen onto the stick. ✦ He tasted it. ✦ It was good! ✦ He knew ✦ he was on to ✦ a good idea! ✦

When you invent something, ✦ you apply for a patent ✦ to protect your idea. ✦ Otherwise, ✦ someone else could claim ✦ that he or she came up with the idea ✦ before you. ✦ It took Frank Epperson ✦ eighteen more years ✦ to apply for his protection patent. ✦ Luckily, he was still ✦ the first person ✦ to have thought of frozen juice ✦ on a stick. ✦ He called his invention ✦ the Epsicle ice pop. ✦ His students renamed his invention ✦ the Popsicle. ✦

Later he invented ✦ the Fudgesicle and Creamsicle. ✦ Frank's patents and brand names ✦ were sold to various companies. ✦ Today, the Good Humor Company owns them. ✦ There are now 30 variations ✦ of the original Epsicle treat. ✦ They come in many flavors, ✦ sizes, ✦ and textures. ✦

Have you ever made your own? ✦ It's so simple! ✦ You can make frozen ✦ orange juice pops. ✦ Or, for a dessert ✦ you can make ✦ the banana chocolate crunch frozen treat. ✦ Peel a banana ✦ and place a craft stick ✦ in one end. ✦ Dip the banana in chocolate syrup ✦ and roll it in nuts. ✦

Another tasty and nutritious ✦ frozen treat ✦ is to blend silken tofu ✦ in a blender ✦ with frozen fruit, ✦ a banana, ✦ and milk. ✦ When it's well blended, ✦ pour it into an ice cube tray ✦ and freeze. ✦ The frozen treat will satisfy ✦ both your hunger and your taste buds. ✦ Keep experimenting! ✦ Perhaps one day ✦ you'll invent a tasty treat ✦ just like Frank did!

Developing Reading Fluency • Gr. 6–8 © 2004 Creative Teaching Press

Popsicles! Popsicles!

What is better on a hot day than a cold Popsicle? The Popsicle was actually invented in the dead of winter in San Francisco, California! An eleven-year-old boy invented it.

On a cold, winter day in 1905, Frank Epperson was drinking punch on his porch. He liked to stir it with a drink stick. Then, Frank went into the house and left his punch outside. The next morning, Frank discovered that his punch had frozen onto the stick. He tasted it. It was good! He knew he was on to a good idea!

When you invent something, you apply for a patent to protect your idea. Otherwise, someone else could claim that he or she came up with the idea before you. It took Frank Epperson eighteen more years to apply for his protection patent. Luckily, he was still the first person to have thought of frozen juice on a stick. He called his invention the Epsicle ice pop. His students renamed his invention the Popsicle.

Later he invented the Fudgesicle and Creamsicle. Frank's patents and brand names were sold to various companies. Today, the Good Humor Company owns them. There are now 30 variations of the original Epsicle treat. They come in many flavors, sizes, and textures.

Have you ever made your own? It's so simple! You can make frozen orange juice pops. Or, for a dessert you can make the banana chocolate crunch frozen treat. Peel a banana and place a craft stick in one end. Dip the banana in chocolate syrup and roll it in nuts.

Another tasty and nutritious frozen treat is to blend silken tofu in a blender with frozen fruit, a banana, and milk. When it's well blended, pour it into an ice cube tray and freeze. The frozen treat will satisfy both your hunger and your taste buds. Keep experimenting! Perhaps one day you'll invent a tasty treat just like Frank did!

Developing Reading Fluency • Gr. 6–8 © 2004 Creative Teaching Press

Phrased Text

The Origin of Crayons

When was the last time ✦ you used crayons? ✦ Maybe you needed them ✦ to add illustrations ✦ to a report ✦ or design something in art class. ✦ You are never too old ✦ to use crayons. ✦ Where did crayons come from? ✦ How are they made? ✦ Crayons are used ✦ in thousands of homes ✦ and classrooms ✦ every single day. ✦

Two cousins, ✦ Edwin Binney and C. Harold Smith, ✦ invented the crayon. ✦ The cousins worked ✦ with Edwin's father, ✦ Joseph Binney, ✦ at his chemical company. ✦ It created a red paint ✦ popular for covering barns ✦ on farms across the U.S. ✦ in the second half ✦ of the 1800s. ✦ The two cousins ✦ formed a partnership ✦ called Binney & Smith. ✦ Together, ✦ they expanded the company's products ✦ to include shoe polish ✦ and printing ink. ✦ To do so, ✦ they expanded ✦ the company's color range ✦ beyond black and red. ✦

They invented wax crayons ✦ to mark crates and barrels. ✦ These were not art crayons, ✦ though. ✦ They contained harmful chemicals— ✦ mainly carbon. ✦ Their goal was to create ✦ a nontoxic, ✦ or safe, ✦ wax crayon ✦ that students could use ✦ for drawing and artwork. ✦ In 1903, ✦ they introduced ✦ their first box ✦ of eight crayons. ✦ Edwin's wife, ✦ Alice, ✦ named them Creole Crayons. ✦ She combined ✦ the French words for *chalk* and *oily*. ✦

That first box of crayons ✦ represented the colors of the rainbow ✦ along with brown and black. ✦ By the year 1949, ✦ another forty colors ✦ had been added ✦ to this rainbow. ✦ A few years later, ✦ in 1958, ✦ they added sixteen more colors. ✦ That brought the total ✦ to the most popular collection ✦ purchased today— ✦ the box of 64 crayons. ✦ Many other variations of color ✦ have since been created, ✦ including multiple skin tones ✦ and fluorescent colors. ✦ However, ✦ that box of 64 ✦ remains the most popular ✦ set of crayons.

Developing Reading Fluency • Gr. 6-8 © 2004 Creative Teaching Press

The Origin of Crayons

When was the last time you used crayons? Maybe you needed them to add illustrations to a report or design something in art class. You are never too old to use crayons. Where did crayons come from? How are they made? Crayons are used in thousands of homes and classrooms every single day.

Two cousins, Edwin Binney and C. Harold Smith, invented the crayon. The cousins worked with Edwin's father, Joseph Binney, at his chemical company. It created a red paint popular for covering barns on farms across the U.S. in the second half of the 1800s. The two cousins formed a partnership called Binney & Smith. Together, they expanded the company's products to include shoe polish and printing ink. To do so, they expanded the company's color range beyond black and red.

They invented wax crayons to mark crates and barrels. These were not art crayons, though. They contained harmful chemicals—mainly carbon. Their goal was to create a nontoxic, or safe, wax crayon that students could use for drawing and artwork. In 1903, they introduced their first box of eight crayons. Edwin's wife, Alice, named them Creole Crayons. She combined the French words for *chalk* and *oily*.

That first box of crayons represented the colors of the rainbow along with brown and black. By the year 1949, another forty colors had been added to this rainbow. A few years later, in 1958, they added sixteen more colors. That brought the total to the most popular collection purchased today—the box of 64 crayons. Many other variations of color have since been created, including multiple skin tones and fluorescent colors. However, that box of 64 remains the most popular set of crayons.

  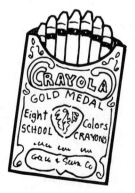

Phrased Text

French Fries

French fries are served ✦ at sports events, ✦ at fast-food restaurants, ✦ and alongside most hamburgers. ✦ They can be sliced thin or thick, ✦ covered with chili, ✦ or sprinkled with salt. ✦ Many are made ✦ from frozen packages, ✦ while some are prepared ✦ fresh to order. ✦ Why are french fries ✦ so popular? ✦ How long have they been around? ✦

In the Netherlands, ✦ thick steak fries ✦ are covered in mayonnaise. ✦ Here in America ✦ we often slice fresh potatoes, ✦ sprinkle them with oil and herbs, ✦ and bake them in an oven. ✦ French fries ✦ are one of the most popular foods ✦ worldwide. ✦ You can travel ✦ to almost any country ✦ and see some variation ✦ of the french fry. ✦ However, ✦ you will not trace the history ✦ of the french fry ✦ back to France. ✦

The french fry ✦ was probably invented in Belgium ✦ Today, in Belgium, ✦ you would be served potatoes ✦ sliced into thick wedges ✦ and placed in a paper cone. ✦ They will also offer you ✦ a variety of toppings— ✦ well beyond the chili fries ✦ common in the United States. ✦

Only Americans ✦ call fried potatoes ✦ french fries. ✦ In England, ✦ they are called chips. ✦ French fries ✦ are most commonly thinly sliced ✦ and served by millions ✦ of fast-food restaurants. ✦ Most people ✦ can identify french fries ✦ just by the scent alone! ✦

If french fries were invented in Belgium, ✦ how did they get to the United States? ✦ Most historians ✦ give credit to Thomas Jefferson. ✦ At a White House dinner ✦ in 1802, ✦ Jefferson served potatoes ✦ in the French manner ✦ after having tasted them in Paris. ✦ In 1918, ✦ American soldiers stationed in France ✦ loved to eat the fried potatoes. ✦ They began calling them ✦ french fries ✦ and wanted to have them ✦ back in America. ✦ Today, there are an average ✦ of four billion pounds ✦ of french fries ✦ sold in the United States ✦ every year! ✦ Those American soldiers ✦ knew a good thing ✦ when they tasted it!

Developing Reading Fluency • Gr. 6–8 © 2004 Creative Teaching Press

French Fries

French fries are served at sports events, at fast-food restaurants, and alongside most hamburgers. They can be sliced thin or thick, covered with chili, or sprinkled with salt. Many are made from frozen packages, while some are prepared fresh to order. Why are french fries so popular? How long have they been around?

In the Netherlands, thick steak fries are covered in mayonnaise. Here in America we often slice fresh potatoes, sprinkle them with oil and herbs, and bake them in an oven. French fries are one of the most popular foods worldwide. You can travel to almost any country and see some variation of the french fry. However, you will not trace the history of the french fry back to France.

The french fry was probably invented in Belgium. Today, in Belgium, you would be served potatoes sliced into thick wedges and placed in a paper cone. They will also offer you a variety of toppings—well beyond the chili fries common in the United States.

Only Americans call fried potatoes french fries. In England, they are called chips. French fries are most commonly thinly sliced and served by millions of fast-food restaurants. Most people can identify french fries just by the scent alone!

If french fries were invented in Belgium, how did they get to the United States? Most historians give credit to Thomas Jefferson. At a White House dinner in 1802, Jefferson served potatoes in the French manner after having tasted them in Paris. In 1918, American soldiers stationed in France loved to eat the fried potatoes. They began calling them french fries and wanted to have them back in America. Today, there are an average of four billion pounds of french fries sold in the United States every year! Those American soldiers knew a good thing when they tasted it!

Developing Reading Fluency • Gr. 6–8 © 2004 Creative Teaching Press

Phrased Text

High-Speed Trains

The oldest high-speed train ✦ in the world ✦ is the Japanese Bullet train. ✦ This train was able ✦ to exceed 200 mph ✦ in 1965. ✦ Today, it can travel faster ✦ than 300 mph. ✦ The high-speed train ✦ connects major cities ✦ that are far apart. ✦ It solves problems, ✦ such as expensive airfares ✦ and massive traffic jams. ✦ It also tends to be better ✦ for the environment ✦ than the alternatives. ✦

In America, ✦ the closest we have to a high-speed train ✦ is the Acela Express. ✦ It connects Boston to New York ✦ and travels at speeds of up to 150 mph. ✦ This is half the speed ✦ of the Japanese trains, ✦ but it far exceeds ✦ the average speed ✦ of other American trains. ✦

In Europe, ✦ high-speed trains ✦ often reach their destination ✦ in about the same amount of time ✦ as an airplane flying ✦ the same route. ✦ France, England, ✦ Germany, Spain, ✦ and Italy ✦ all have high-speed trains. ✦

In California, ✦ there are plans to build ✦ a 700-mile track ✦ for a high-speed train ✦ that would stretch ✦ from Sacramento to San Diego. ✦ It would pass ✦ through San Francisco, ✦ the Central Valley, ✦ and Los Angeles. ✦ It could cost less ✦ to take the two-and-a-half-hour ride ✦ from Los Angeles to San Francisco ✦ than it would to buy the gas ✦ to drive there. ✦

High-speed trains ✦ benefit more than the passenger. ✦ They create jobs ✦ to build and run the railway. ✦ Because the rail lines ✦ tend to run through ✦ less populated areas, ✦ they often bring people ✦ and businesses ✦ to areas where there are currently few. ✦ However, the job is not a small one. ✦ Even if plans continue ✦ for the California train, ✦ it is unlikely to be completed ✦ until the year 2020.

Developing Reading Fluency • Gr. 6–8 © 2004 Creative Teaching Press

High-Speed Trains

The oldest high-speed train in the world is the Japanese Bullet train. This train was able to exceed 200 mph in 1965. Today, it can travel faster than 300 mph. The high-speed train connects major cities that are far apart. It solves problems, such as expensive airfares and massive traffic jams. It also tends to be better for the environment than the alternatives.

In America, the closest we have to a high-speed train is the Acela Express. It connects Boston to New York and travels at speeds of up to 150 mph. This is half the speed of the Japanese trains, but far exceeds the average speed of other American trains.

In Europe, high-speed trains often reach their destination in about the same amount of time as an airplane flying the same route. France, England, Germany, Spain, and Italy all have high-speed trains.

In California, there are plans to build a 700-mile track for a high-speed train that would stretch from Sacramento to San Diego. It would pass through San Francisco, the Central Valley, and Los Angeles. It could cost less to take the two-and-a-half-hour ride from Los Angeles to San Francisco than it would to buy the gas to drive there.

High-speed trains benefit more than the passenger. They create jobs to build and run the railway. Because the rail lines tend to run through less populated areas, they often bring people and businesses to areas where there are currently few. However, the job is not a small one. Even if plans continue for the California train, it is unlikely to be completed until the year 2020.

Developing Reading Fluency • Gr. 6–8 © 2004 Creative Teaching Press

Phrased Text

Sparta and Athens

Ancient Greece was a busy place. ✦ It consisted of many larger city-states ✦ and smaller villages and towns. ✦ The people spoke the same language, ✦ worshipped the same gods, ✦ and shared similar tastes ✦ in clothing and food. ✦ But it was not one unified country, ✦ and there were some big differences ✦ between the city-states. ✦

Each city-state ✦ had its own system of government ✦ and ways of doing things. ✦ Perhaps nowhere ✦ were the differences as great ✦ as between the two large city-states ✦ of Sparta and Athens. ✦

Spartans loved to fight. ✦ They admired bravery and strength ✦ over anything else. ✦ Young boys started training early ✦ for battle. ✦ Being tough and using weapons ✦ was as much a part of school ✦ as survival skills. ✦ The Spartans, ✦ once almost defeated ✦ by a village they had annexed, ✦ developed a highly structured military state. ✦ Every free male ✦ served in the military. ✦ Until the age of thirty, ✦ even the married men ✦ lived entirely with the army. ✦ After the age of thirty, ✦ they could live ✦ with their families, ✦ but they continued to serve ✦ with the military ✦ until they were sixty years old. ✦ Spartans gave everything ✦ to support their city. ✦ To do this, ✦ they lived simply, ✦ and they kept slaves. ✦ It was the slaves ✦ who did the farming, ✦ giving a portion of the food ✦ to the Spartan and his family ✦ and keeping a portion for themselves. ✦ Today, ✦ when we say someone ✦ lives a spartan existence, ✦ we mean he or she keeps only ✦ what is needed and nothing more. ✦

The lives of the Athenians were much different. ✦ The people of Athens ✦ were mostly free citizens. ✦ Although they used slaves ✦ in the early portion of their history, ✦ they soon found ✦ that the differences between rich and poor ✦ created an instability ✦ that would soon lead to war. ✦ They spent a long period ✦ sweeping various rulers ✦ in and out of power ✦ until at last ✦ they had a democratic system ✦ where most of the male members ✦ of the city-state ✦ were citizens who could vote. ✦ At the heart of this system ✦ was the belief ✦ that an ignorant people ✦ could soon be persuaded ✦ to vote badly, ✦ so they developed excellent schools ✦ that taught reading, ✦ writing, and math ✦ as well as art and music. ✦ Most girls did not attend. ✦ They learned ✦ to run the home instead. ✦ But some girls did learn ✦ to read and write at home. ✦

The two city-states often fought. ✦ It was generally agreed ✦ that Sparta ✦ had the better military ✦ and Athens ✦ was the cultural and educational center ✦ of Greece. ✦ Still, ✦ when the Persians ✦ threatened to invade, ✦ the two city-states ✦ did what was in both ✦ of their best interests—✦ they finally learned to work together.

Developing Reading Fluency • Gr. 6–8 © 2004 Creative Teaching Press

Sparta and Athens

Ancient Greece was a busy place. It consisted of many larger city-states and smaller villages and towns. The people spoke the same language, worshipped the same gods, and shared similar tastes in clothing and food. But it was not one unified country, and there were some big differences between the city-states.

Each city-state had its own system of government and ways of doing things. Perhaps nowhere were the differences as great as between the two large city-states of Sparta and Athens.

Spartans loved to fight. They admired bravery and strength over anything else. Young boys started training early for battle. Being tough and using weapons was as much a part of school as survival skills. The Spartans, once almost defeated by a village they had annexed, developed a highly structured military state. Every free male served in the military. Until the age of thirty, even the married men lived entirely with the army. After the age of thirty, they could live with their families, but they continued to serve with the military until they were sixty years old. Spartans gave everything to support their city. To do this, they lived simply, and they kept slaves. It was the slaves who did the farming, giving a portion of the food to the Spartan and his family and keeping a portion for themselves. Today, when we say someone lives a spartan existence, we mean he or she keeps only what is needed and nothing more.

The lives of the Athenians were much different. The people of Athens were mostly free citizens. Although they used slaves in the early portion of their history, they soon found that the differences between rich and poor created an instability that would soon lead to war. They spent a long period sweeping various rulers in and out of power until at last they had a democratic system where most of the male members of the city-state were citizens who could vote. At the heart of this system was the belief that an ignorant people could soon be persuaded to vote badly, so they developed excellent schools that taught reading, writing, and math, as well as art and music. Most girls did not attend. They learned to run the home instead. But some girls did learn to read and write at home.

The two city-states often fought. It was generally agreed that Sparta had the better military and Athens was the cultural and educational center of Greece. Still, when the Persians threatened to invade, the two city-states did what was in both of their best interests—they finally learned to work together.

Phrased Text

Leo Africanus

Around the time of Christopher Columbus, ✦ a student was born ✦ in Granada, Spain. ✦ His birth name ✦ was Al-Hassan Ibn-Mohammed ✦ Al-Wezaz Al-Fasi, ✦ but he is remembered ✦ as Leo Africanus. ✦ He was an Arab ✦ living in southern Spain ✦ in the Spanish Moor community. ✦ His father was a landowner. ✦ His uncle was an ambassador ✦ as well as an excellent speaker ✦ and poet. ✦ The boy would grow up, ✦ travel throughout Northern Africa, ✦ be presented as a slave ✦ to the Pope, ✦ and eventually write ✦ A History and Description of Africa. ✦ The book ✦ provided Europeans with the best information ✦ of the area for centuries. ✦

When Leo was still quite young, ✦ Granada returned to Spanish rule ✦ for the first time in 700 years. ✦ Leo's family ✦ could have stayed ✦ and become Spanish citizens. ✦ Instead, they chose to move ✦ to Northern Africa. ✦ They settled around Morocco and Fez. ✦ At the time, ✦ this area ✦ was the center of education ✦ for Northern Africa. ✦ There were famous libraries. ✦ Students from all areas ✦ of Islam ✦ traveled there to study. ✦ Young Leo studied grammar, ✦ poetry, ✦ rhetoric, ✦ philosophy, ✦ history, ✦ and Arabic. ✦ He was an excellent student. ✦

Because he was so well educated, ✦ he acted as a judge, ✦ or lawyer, ✦ to a number of smaller towns ✦ in his early teens. ✦ He was only 15 ✦ when he earned a salary ✦ as a judge ✦ for the town of Medea. ✦ He also was responsible ✦ for writing and carrying messages ✦ between some of the larger cities ✦ of the area. ✦ He was soon very well traveled. ✦

He was in his mid-twenties ✦ when he was captured and enslaved ✦ by a group of pirates. ✦ When they discovered ✦ they had a man of learning, ✦ they took him to Pope Leo X ✦ in the hope that they might be forgiven ✦ for a lifetime of crime. ✦ Pope Leo X ✦ changed the African traveler's ✦ name to Leo. ✦ (Leo's knowledge of Africa ✦ gave him his last name of Africanus.) ✦ Pope Leo X ✦ immediately freed him ✦ and offered him a large salary ✦ to stay. ✦ Leo soon "converted" ✦ to Christianity, ✦ but it is generally agreed ✦ that he did so ✦ just to gain favor. ✦ Late in his life ✦ he would return to Islam. ✦

He taught Arabic, ✦ learned Italian, ✦ brushed up on his Latin, ✦ and soon began to write ✦ the book for which ✦ he is famous today. ✦ He used the libraries of Rome ✦ and his personal journals ✦ to record, mostly correctly, ✦ a detailed description of Africa. ✦ It remained the primary source ✦ of information ✦ about the continent ✦ for hundreds of years.

Developing Reading Fluency • Gr. 6–8 © 2004 Creative Teaching Press

Leo Africanus

Around the time of Christopher Columbus, a student was born in Granada, Spain. His birth name was Al-Hassan Ibn-Mohammed Al-Wezaz Al-Fasi, but he is remembered as Leo Africanus. He was an Arab living in southern Spain in the Spanish Moor community. His father was a landowner. His uncle was an ambassador as well as an excellent speaker and poet. The boy would grow up, travel throughout Northern Africa, be presented as a slave to the Pope, and eventually write A History and Description of Africa. The book provided Europeans with the best information of the area for centuries.

When Leo was still quite young, Granada returned to Spanish rule for the first time in 700 years. Leo's family could have stayed and become Spanish citizens. Instead, they chose to move to Northern Africa. They settled around Morocco and Fez. At the time, this area was the center of education for Northern Africa. There were famous libraries. Students from all areas of Islam traveled there to study. Young Leo studied grammar, poetry, rhetoric, philosophy, history, and Arabic. He was an excellent student.

Because he was so well educated, he acted as a judge, or lawyer, to a number of smaller towns in his early teens. He was only 15 when he earned a salary as a judge for the town of Medea. He also was responsible for writing and carrying messages between some of the larger cities of the area. He was soon very well traveled.

He was in his mid-twenties when he was captured and enslaved by a group of pirates. When they discovered they had a man of learning, they took him to Pope Leo X in the hope that they might be forgiven for a lifetime of crime. Pope Leo X changed the African traveler's name to Leo. (Leo's knowledge of Africa gave him his last name of Africanus.) Pope Leo X immediately freed him and offered him a large salary to stay. Leo soon "converted" to Christianity, but it is generally agreed that he did so just to gain favor. Late in his life he would return to Islam.

He taught Arabic, learned Italian, brushed up on his Latin, and soon began to write the book for which he is famous today. He used the libraries of Rome and his personal journals to record, mostly correctly, a detailed description of Africa. It remained the primary source of information about the continent for hundreds of years.

Developing Reading Fluency • Gr. 6-8 © 2004 Creative Teaching Press

Phrased Text

Reader's Theater

Reader's Theater is a motivating and exciting way for students to mature into fluent and expressive readers. Reader's Theater does not use any props, costumes, or materials other than the script, which allows the focus to stay on fluent and expressive reading. The "actors" must tell the story using only their voices and rely on their tone of voice, expression, phrasing, and fluency to express the story to the audience. Students are reading for a purpose, which highly motivates them because they take on the roles of characters and bring the characters to life through voice inflection. Each Reader's Theater script is designed for a group of four students. However, the scripts can be modified, if necessary. For example, students can double-up on roles to incorporate paired reading.

Strategies: repeated oral reading for groups of four; choral reading; paired reading

Materials
- highlighters
- colored file folders

Directions

1. Make four copies of each play. (Each play is several pages long.) Staple the pages together along the left side of the script (not the top). Highlight a different character's part on each script.

2. Gather four folders of the same color for each play. Put one copy of the script in each folder. Write the title of the play and the name of the highlighted character (e.g., Aaron, Emily) on the front of each folder.

3. Divide the class into groups of four. Give each student in a group the same color folder (containing the same script).

4. Have students first read the entire script. (Research supports having students read all of the roles for the first day or two to fully comprehend the story.) Then, have each student choose which part he or she will perform, or assign each student a part. Have students switch folders so that each student has the script with the highlighted character's part that he or she will play. **Note:** "The Surprise in the Attic" (page 70) is left open for prediction. Invite groups to compose an ending for the script.

5. Invite students to perform their play for the whole class, another group, a buddy class, or their parents.

Extension

Invite students to write a Reader's Theater script to be used with four readers. Type the script, and follow the five steps above using the script created by the students.

The Great Bag Party

Characters: Aaron   Josh
                  Emily   Narrator

Narrator

Josh and Aaron decided to throw a huge party for all their friends. Aaron's little sister, Emily, was going to help out. It was going to be quite unusual. None of the friends had a birthday to celebrate. It wasn't a special holiday. In fact, it was a party for no particular reason at all. They were all seated at Josh's dining room table, making their final plans.

Aaron

Josh, did you send out all the invitations?

Josh

I sure did! I sent them all out three days ago. Everyone should have gotten them by now. We should start getting some calls from people who will RSVP anyday now.

Emily

How many people did we end up inviting?

Josh

I mailed 42 invitations, not including us of course. Hopefully, most of the people will want to come.

Emily

Our invitation did make it clear that it's a project party, right?

Developing Reading Fluency • Gr. 6–8 © 2004 Creative Teaching Press

The Great Bag Party

Aaron

Definitely. It explained exactly what we planned together two weeks ago. Don't you remember? You decorated the invitations yourself!

Emily

Of course I remember. I just wanted to know if you made any changes.

Aaron

Of course not. You made the perfect invitations! Now, let's get on with our planning. How many canvas bags do we have?

Josh

The last time I counted we had 34 canvas bags, which means that we won't have enough if everyone actually shows up. That's also not including the bags we'll need. Peterson drugs is donating the bags.

Emily

I just got my allowance. I could buy another bag or two with that. I think I saw an ad that showed them on sale this week. We could luck out!

Josh

Good idea! While you're checking on that, we'll see how many bottles of fabric paint we have.

Aaron

It looks like we'll have enough paint since we can just put it on paper plates and share. That invitation did say to bring a gently used and greatly loved stuffed animal along with two books to the party, didn't it?

Developing Reading Fluency • Gr. 6–8 © 2004 Creative Teaching Press

The Great Bag Party

Narrator

Emily was digging into her piggy bank, but she turned around to answer Aaron before Josh could.

Emily

I did put that on the invitations. I even put a star next to those things so our guests wouldn't forget them. But we have extras just in case.

Narrator

The three friends continued their tasks. Emily counted her money and discovered that she did have enough money to buy three more bags due to the low sales price. Josh was organizing the fabric paint by color and amount. Aaron was busy checking off things from the list they created.

Emily

We're all set then! All we need are some guests, snack foods, and music! I just can't wait!

Aaron

I'll ask my parents if we can go to the store and buy some cookies, chips and salsa, and grapes.

Emily

I can make some chocolate chip cookies myself. You know I make better cookies than anything dad could buy at the store!

Aaron

Sounds great! Josh, do you think you could ask your mom to make her famous fruit salad?

Developing Reading Fluency • Gr. 6–8 © 2004 Creative Teaching Press

The Great Bag Party

Josh
Sure! We could also order some pizzas just in case we all get hungry. Let's check your list to see what we still need to do before the party.

Narrator
After checking the list, Aaron and Emily went home. They agreed to meet two hours before the party to organize their materials for the First Annual Project Party. If all went well, they were planning on making it something they did at least once a year. They were hoping that all the guests would have so much fun that they'd try making a party of their own one day. Before long, there would be project parties all over the country!

Emily
Well, are we all ready for a party? I heard back from 35 people who plan on coming! This is going to be fabulous!

Aaron
So that makes a total of 38 bags we'll have to donate to the homeless shelter. My parents will be so excited! They said that there are sad, lonely students who live there with their parents for weeks or even months at a time. These bags will surely cheer them up!

Narrator
They arranged ten tables and placed bags and fabric paints on each table. Then they ordered the pizzas and waited for their friends and guests to arrive.

Emily
They're here!

Developing Reading Fluency • Gr. 6–8 © 2004 Creative Teaching Press

The Great Bag Party

Narrator

Almost everyone arrived on time, so the party was underway. The three friends decided to let Josh explain their plan.

Josh

Thank you all for coming to our mysterious Project Party! We're so excited to have you join us. Each of you will decorate a bag, put your stuffed animal and book inside, and deliver the bag to a local shelter for children to enjoy.

Emily

We all know that in hard times, there's nothing better than having a comfort item to hang on to.

Aaron

And, since we all love reading, we thought giving a book or two to each student with the stuffed animal would be a great idea.

Narrator

A few of their friends started clapping. After only a few seconds, everyone was clapping and excited to start the project. Emily explained how the tables were arranged. Then the doorbell rang.

Josh

That must be the pizza!

Narrator

Everyone was so busy laughing and talking that they didn't even hear him. Within hours they had 38 beautiful bags stuffed with animals and books ready for delivery!

Developing Reading Fluency • Gr. 6-8 © 2004 Creative Teaching Press

Reader's Theater

The Surprise in the Attic

Characters: Garrett   Kendra
Sandy   Narrator

Garrett
Are we there yet? This is taking forever!

Narrator
Kendra and Garrett were visiting their uncle in his new home. He had just moved into a cabin about seven hours north of them. Their mom, Sandy, had driven them there.

Sandy
Yes, Garrett. We're almost there. It's only another five miles or so. Look at all the beautiful trees. The leaves are changing color!

Kendra
Wow! I see so many that are bright orange, yellow, and even red!

Garrett
Where? Oh, now I see them. They are pretty. Why don't we have trees like that at our house?

Sandy
That's because we live by the coast. The leaves don't change with the seasons in the southwest as much as they do in the northern parts of the state. Here we are!

Kendra
Hooray! I can't wait to see Uncle!

Developing Reading Fluency • Gr. 6–8 © 2004 Creative Teaching Press

The Surprise in the Attic

Garrett

Let's go get him!

Narrator

While Sandy was busy getting their bags out of the car, Kendra and Garrett ran to the door and began knocking. Their uncle greeted them with a hug and helped Sandy carry in the bags.

Kendra

I want a tour. Will you show me around your new place?

Narrator

Their uncle walked them through the entryway, through the kitchen, into the dining room, and to the living room. He then took them up the stairs to show them the two bedrooms.

Kendra

This is a great place, Uncle! Can I sleep in the room upstairs?

Garrett

I want to build a fort! Mom, can we build a fort downstairs while Kendra sleeps upstairs?

Sandy

I don't see why not. Let's get started.

Narrator

Since it was already dark when they arrived, they had just enough time to build their fort, unpack their suitcases, and eat dinner. Then they were off to bed. Four hours into sleep, Kendra heard a strange sound coming from above her head.

Developing Reading Fluency • Gr. 6–8 © 2004 Creative Teaching Press

Reader's Theater

The Surprise in the Attic

Kendra (screaming)
HELP! HELP! Somebody help me!

Narrator
Everyone jumped out of bed and went running up to Kendra's room.

Sandy
What's wrong? Why did you scream? You woke everybody up.

Garrett
Why did you scream and wake me up?

Kendra
I heard a weird noise! It was right up there! It woke me up! I'm not sleeping in here anymore. Somebody's up there on the roof!

Sandy
There isn't anyone on the roof. You were probably just having a bad dream. Let's all go back to sleep.

Narrator
Just then, the noise happened again.

Garrett
Whoa! What was that? Mom, I'm scared! Who's on Uncle's roof?

Sandy
That didn't sound like a person at all. It's probably just a possum or cat running across the top of the house.

Kendra
Get me out of here!

Developing Reading Fluency • Gr. 6–8 © 2004 Creative Teaching Press

The Surprise in the Attic

Garrett

Me, too!

Narrator

Their uncle was already outside with a flashlight, looking for something on the roof. He came back in to tell everyone that they were safe and that there was nothing on the roof. They could all go back to bed.

Kendra

There it is again! It's there! I hear it!

Sandy

It must be in the attic. It's probably just a mouse or something.

Garrett

That's no big deal. I have a pet rat. You do, too. Relax. Let's go back to bed.

Kendra

I want Uncle to check it now. I can't go back to bed until I know what it is.

Sandy

There's a chair right there. I'll check for myself. Then you can both go to sleep and get some rest.

Garrett

Be careful!

Narrator

Sandy opened the latch to the attic. She poked her head up to take a peek. Then she asked for the flashlight. All of a sudden, they heard the noise again and Sandy nearly fell off the chair!

Developing Reading Fluency • Gr. 6–8 © 2004 Creative Teaching Press

Reader's Theater

The Surprise in the Attic

Kendra

There it is again! Mom—are you all right? What's up there? It's still there, isn't it?

Narrator

All of a sudden a bird flew into the room! Everyone started screaming and running!

Kendra

Watch out!

Garrett

How'd a bird get into your attic? How are we ever going to get it out of the house?

Sandy

Hold on! I've heard of this happening before. I know what we can do. Garrett, go open the front door and turn on the porch light. Kendra, turn off all the lights in the house.

Kendra

But then we won't be able to see! The bird could attack us!

Sandy

It's just scared. It wants out. I have no idea how it got in there, but it wants out. If we sit quietly in the dark, the bird will fly toward the light and go out the front door.

Kendra

Do you think that will really work?

(left open for prediction)

Developing Reading Fluency • Gr. 6–8 © 2004 Creative Teaching Press

The Radio Contest

Characters: DJ Rob Ray   Michelle
              Danny   Narrator

DJ Rob Ray

Hello, all of you out there in radio land! It's time for our Rockin' Boppin' Radio Contest here at WSHI! I'm going to take the 16th caller after I play the song "When I Was Young." As soon as the song ends, the 16th caller will answer a funny trivia question.

Narrator

DJ Rob Ray put on the song. He read the trivia question and began laughing. He didn't think anyone would get it right. People all around the county were trying to call in. They were hoping to just push the redial button over and over until they got through. Meanwhile, in two different homes, Danny and Michelle were each trying to get through.

Michelle

How does anyone ever win one of these radio contests anyway?

Danny

Why am I even trying to win? I don't even know what the prize is. It's usually a pair of concert tickets, but how do I know if I even like the band?

Michelle

I'm probably just wasting my time, but now that I've started I just can't give up! I really should be doing my homework instead.

Developing Reading Fluency • Gr. 6–8 © 2004 Creative Teaching Press

Reader's Theater

The Radio Contest

Narrator

The song was just ending. Meanwhile, Danny and Michelle, along with hundreds of other WSHI radio listeners, were trying to dial in to the station, hoping to be the 16th caller.

DJ Rob Ray

Well, well, well. That was the contest song. Let's see who I have on the line. We're almost to caller 16! Here we go! Hello?

Michelle

Hello? Hello? Did I really get through? Is this DJ Rob Ray?

DJ Rob Ray

It sure is!

Michelle

Am I caller 16? Did I win the tickets?

DJ Rob Ray

Hold on there. Did I mention anything about tickets being the prize? You are caller 16, but you haven't won anything quite yet.

Michelle

It's really me? I won? Is this a trick?

DJ Rob Ray

The only thing you've won so far is the chance to talk with me on live radio. While that may be a great reward in itself, you do have a chance to win something else if you can answer my trivia question correctly. Are you ready?

Michelle

Am I ready? I've been trying to call in at the right time for your contests for months now! I can't believe it!

Developing Reading Fluency • Gr. 6–8 © 2004 Creative Teaching Press

The Radio Contest

DJ Rob Ray

Hold on one second. To all you other callers out there—don't give up. If this little lady has any trouble, I'm going to let one of you try to help her. So . . . keep your calls coming in!

Narrator

Michelle was still trying to catch her breath. She couldn't believe she had actually gotten through to the radio station.

DJ Rob Ray

Here's your question. Before you answer, remember that you only get one guess. Then I'll take another caller. Are you ready?

Michelle

I'm ready.

DJ Rob Ray

Here's your question: What were some of the most popular snack treats in the late 1800s and early 1900s?

Narrator

Meanwhile, Danny was still trying to get through on his phone at home.

Danny

I know this answer! I just did a report on that!

Michelle

Well, I think that's when candy bars were first invented. I'll say the candy bar.

Developing Reading Fluency • Gr. 6–8 © 2004 Creative Teaching Press

The Radio Contest

DJ Rob Ray

Oh, I'm so sorry! Your answer is wrong. But today is Try Again Tuesday! I'm going to take the next caller. That person will help you try again. If you can both figure it out, then you'll get to share in the prize. Ready?

Narrator

Although Michelle was very disappointed, at least she had one more chance. Who knew what the prize was anyway? She just wanted to win.

DJ Rob Ray

Hello, you're the next caller. Can you be of some help to Michelle?

Danny

Hello? I think I know the answer. I just did a report on street vendors of the late 1800s.

DJ Rob Ray

What were among the most popular snack treats in the late 1800s and early 1900s?

Danny

I think they were popcorn balls!

DJ Rob Ray

Unbelievable! I can't believe you knew that!

Danny

You mean I'm right? I won? I won the contest?

DJ Rob Ray

Well, sort of. This was Try Again Tuesday, which means that Michelle got to try again with the help of another caller. That caller was you!

Developing Reading Fluency • Gr. 6–8 © 2004 Creative Teaching Press

The Radio Contest

Danny

So I helped Michelle win?

DJ Rob Ray

You sure did! Your reward for helping a fellow WSHI caller is to share the prize!

Narrator

Hundreds of disappointed radio listeners stopped calling in. They waited to hear what the mysterious prize would be.

DJ Rob Ray

In order to collect your prize, you must guess it from the following rhyme:
> *It has two wheels and goes very fast.*
> *On the freeway it won't be last!*

Danny

No way! You've got to be kidding me! Did I win the motorcycle for myself or are we sharing one?

DJ Rob Ray

You each get your very own! How's that for a radio prize? That might be our best prize ever!

Michelle

But I don't even know how to drive a . . . what was it?

Developing Reading Fluency • Gr. 6–8 © 2004 Creative Teaching Press

The Safari Ride

Characters: Fred   Max
               Erin   Safari Sue

Safari Sue

Welcome aboard our safari truck! My name's Safari Sue. I'll be your tour guide as we travel through this natural preserve. Along our path, watch out for many unique animals roaming in native-like habitats. Keep your hands and feet inside! You never know when one of our residents may be hungry!

Erin

I'm so excited you planned this trip for us, Fred. The pictures I've seen look like we're really going on an African safari!

Max

Whoa! It looks like we're in for a bumpy ride!

Fred

Let's get the camera ready. I don't want to miss any funny shots of the animals!

Safari Sue

Well now! What have we here? Our first stop has brought us to the Giraffe Habitat. Hold on to your cameras. They've been known to reach right in and take a few!

Max

Look! That giraffe can reach all the way to the top of the tree!

Developing Reading Fluency • Gr. 6–8 © 2004 Creative Teaching Press

The Safari Ride

Safari Sue

As you may already know, the giraffe has the same number of vertebrae in its neck as other mammals. They are just really big and stretched out. What you may not know is that a giraffe's kick can actually kill a lion! Indeed, giraffes are one of the largest and strongest animals on earth. They are also among the most peaceful, so you probably won't see any kicking today.

Erin

Hey look! It's an ox pecker bird! They help the giraffes by eating the bugs off their backs.

Max

Gross! Is that similar to how some birds help clean a crocodile's teeth?

Erin

It's the same basic idea of one animal helping another. Hang on! This is one bumpy ride. We must be off to the next habitat.

Fred

I hope I don't start feeling queasy. I had no idea it would be this bumpy!

Safari Sue

We're about to come upon the Rhino Room. As you can see, we're in luck this morning. Since it's so early, we'll have a chance to see more animals than usual. If you look off to your right, you'll see our biggest rhino.

Max

Check out that horn! I'd bet he can do some damage to a lion, too. That looks sharp!

Developing Reading Fluency • Gr. 6–8 © 2004 Creative Teaching Press

Reader's Theater

The Safari Ride

Erin

Actually, since they are vegetarians, it's very unlikely that they would bother a lion. They prefer to roam the grasslands.

Safari Sue

Hang on! We're off again!

Fred

Here comes your favorite, Max!

Max

Oh! It's just like I've seen in my magazines and books. What kind of elephant is it—Asian or African?

Erin

I think it's an African elephant since it has such big ears. I remember reading that the Asian elephants have smaller ears. Oh! Listen! You can hear them. I wonder if they're saying hello to us to telling us to go away.

Safari Sue

Moving on . . . our next stop will be at the home of the King of the Beasts!

Fred

Now you're talking! That's what I've been waiting for. When I was in fourth grade, I did a report on lions. I still remember that report. I got an A on it!

Safari Sue

As you can see, the lions are lounging around today. I love visiting the lions! You never know what you'll see or hear. Let's see what you already know about lions. Who can tell me a fact?

Fred

They're carnivores just like me!

Developing Reading Fluency • Gr. 6–8 © 2004 Creative Teaching Press

The Safari Ride

Safari Sue

Very good! The only difference is that you use a fork and a knife and they use their extremely powerful jaws. Does anyone else have something to share about lions?

Max

I know that they live in groups called prides and they are social cats. My cat at home doesn't care much about me, but lions are social.

Safari Sue

You're right! That's a good comparison to your pet cat. Any other facts out there?

Erin

Isn't it also true that they are Africa's largest carnivores?

Safari Sue

Wow! We have a smart bunch riding with us today. You're right, too. Well, let me see if there's anything else I know that I can share with you. I think the most important thing for me to remind you of is that they are quickly disappearing in number. They are losing their habitat which is life threatening for this species.

Fred

Did you hear that? I think maybe the King is speaking to us.

Safari Sue

Well, that's the end of our tour today. I hope you've enjoyed seeing some of Africa's amazing animals on our safari. Let's go back the way we came so we can visit each habitat one more time!

Developing Reading Fluency • Gr. 6–8 © 2004 Creative Teaching Press

Intervention Activities

Every section in this book can be used throughout the year to teach, guide, practice, and reinforce reading with phrasing and fluency, which will improve students' reading comprehension. The following activities provide additional practice and instruction for those students who need more help with the strategies that will help them improve their reading fluency. Assess students' stage of fluency by referring to the chart on page 7.

Use the following activities with "robotic readers" to help them be successful. The activities in this section will help students focus on the following strategies: phrased reading, automaticity with high-frequency words and phrases, recognition of what fluency sounds like at the listening level, and active listening.

Each activity includes an objective, a materials list, and step-by-step instructions. The activities are best suited to individualized instruction or very small groups. The activities can be adapted for use with larger groups or a whole-class setting in some cases.

Phrasing Cards

Strategies: explicit phrasing; automaticity with common phrases; modeled reading; repeated reading

Objective: Each student will practice reading the phrases with increasing speed and accuracy.

Materials
- Phrasing Cards (pages 86–89)
- Reading Rate Progress Plotter (page 90)
- card stock
- scissors
- 2 binder rings
- timer

Directions

1. Photocopy both sets of cards on card stock. Laminate the cards for durability. The first set consists of two- to three-word phrases. The second set has mostly four-word phrases. Use Set 1 before Set 2. Your goal is to have students read four- to five-word phrases by the end of fifth grade.

2. Cut apart the cards, and hole-punch them. Put them on two different rings—Set 1 and Set 2—for fast flipping.

3. Photocopy the Reading Rate Progress Plotter for each student.

4. Get a timer to keep track of the time it takes a student to read the set of cards most appropriate for him or her.

5. Call the student over to a quiet space in the room for one-on-one instruction.

6. **Do NOT review the phrases or model before beginning this activity.** Your goal is to determine the student's baseline phrasing ability and then scaffold the learning.

7. When you are ready to start, begin the timer and flip the phrasing cards at a steady pace. Try to maintain this pace with all students each time. (For this reason, it is best not to use adult volunteers for this activity.)

8. As you flip, try your best to count the number of phrases the student actually reads word by word—not in phrases. This will help you discover the relationship between phrasing and speed for each student.

9. Record the student's reading rate and the approximate number of phrases read as phrases (not word by word).

10. Immediately **after** the student finishes, go through and model the reading of one phrase at a time. Have the student repeat after you. Repeat this step one more time.

11. Repeat the ten steps listed above every day for ten consecutive days. Move the student from Set 1 to Set 2 when he or she can read each phrase in under 4 seconds.

Intervention Activities

Phrasing Cards: Set 1
(2- to 3-word common phrases)

you and I	the people
he called me	one more time
not now	sit down
now and then	each of us
he has it	in the end
but not me	we were here
all day long	it's about time
which way	some people
what happened next	right now
put it there	going under
help me out	give it away
it never happened	in the beginning

Developing Reading Fluency • Gr. 6–8 © 2004 Creative Teaching Press

Phrasing Cards: Set 1
(2- to 3-word common phrases)

in each case	for these reasons
over time	just in time
and so on	have been able
in other words	for example
as a result	a couple of
as with many	may one day
in that place	it is likely
just too soon	could already see
he couldn't see	I think so
close the door	I miss you
on my side	a good thought
because of that	do it often

Developing Reading Fluency • Gr. 6–8 © 2004 Creative Teaching Press

Intervention Activities

Phrasing Cards: Set 2
(4-word common phrases)

end of the day	are among the best
and in the end	as if he were
on the way back	once upon a time
all of a sudden	a new way of
on top of the	she could see that
he tried to think	at the next place
in the first place	just could not understand
the best way to	so in the end
as big as the	the very next day
in a long time	now is the time
a number of people	once in a while
what they will do	more than the other

Developing Reading Fluency • Gr. 6–8 © 2004 Creative Teaching Press

Phrasing Cards: Set 2
(4-word common phrases)

in so many ways	but on the way
a list of ways	what have you learned
so they could see	she thought about it
go through with it	about to get caught
get over the fact	a couple of times
to see how they	they could not decide
which do you think	compare the two ways
on the other hand	later on that day
the interesting thing is	the main reason why
in such a hurry	put part of it
in addition to that	once there was a
tried to find it	and then what happened

Developing Reading Fluency • Gr. 6–8 © 2004 Creative Teaching Press

Intervention Activities

Reading Rate Progress Plotter

Name				
Date	Reading Rate	Rubic Score	Number of Correct Phrases	Growth?

Name				
Date	Reading Rate	Rubic Score	Number of Correct Phrases	Growth?

Developing Reading Fluency • Gr. 6–8 © 2004 Creative Teaching Press

Roll a Phrase

Strategies: explicit phrasing; repeated reading; phrases in writing

Objective: Each student will dictate and/or write five sentences with the rolled phrases. The student will break up the sentences will be broken up into phrased, meaningful chunks.

Materials
- Roll a Phrase dice (page 92)
- dry erase board or paper
- dry erase marker or pencils

Directions

1. Photocopy the dice on page 92. Cut out the dice, and laminate them for durability. Form the dice by taping the sides together.

2. Invite one or two students to work with you in a quiet area of the room.

3. Model the activity by rolling the dice. Say the phrases that are rolled in a clear phrased voice. Make up a sentence or sentences using the phrases. Model correct phrasing. Have students repeat your sentence.

4. Invite one student to roll the dice. That student will then say the rolled phrases. If the student does not use correct phrasing, model and have the student repeat. Next, have the student say a sentence with the phrases in it. Repeat the student's sentence exactly the way he or she said it (with or without phrasing). Your goal is to train the student's ear to hear the phrased chunks within the spoken sentences.

5. Continue a few times until it appears the student can hear and speak in phrases.

6. Give the student a piece of paper or a dry erase board. Have him or her roll the dice again. Then, have the student write down a sentence in phrased chunks using the rolled phrases.

7. Read aloud the student's sentence.

Roll a Phrase

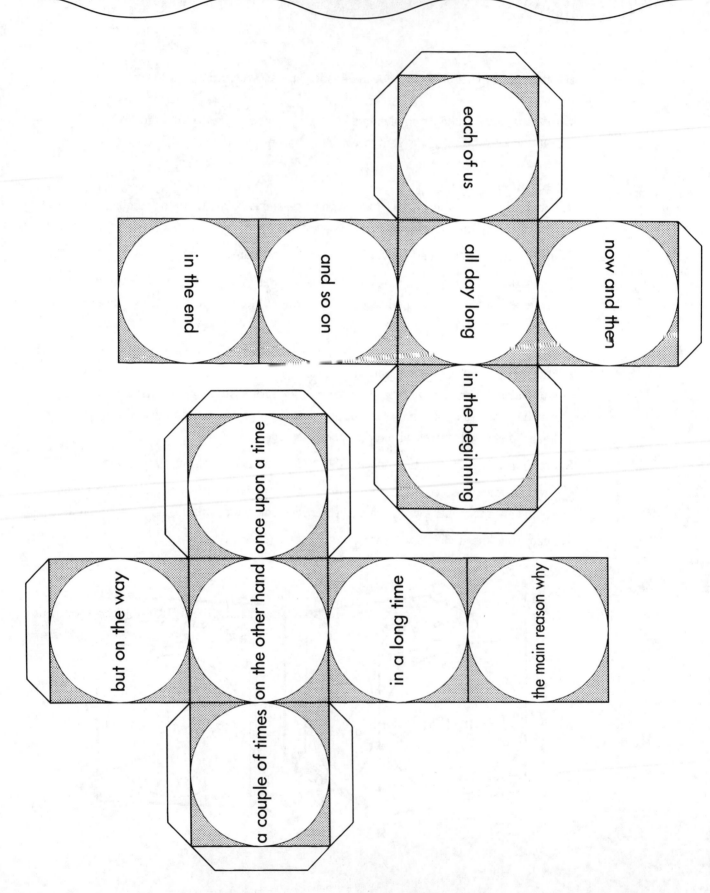

Developing Reading Fluency • Gr. 6–8 © 2004 Creative Teaching Press

Chop It Up!

Strategies: explicit phrasing; repeated reading; choral reading; language experience

Objective: Each student will be able to reconstruct his or her own dictated sentences, which have been cut into phrases by the teacher. The student will then be able to read his or her own sentences with phrasing and fluency.

Materials
- black marker
- strips of paper
- scissors

Directions

1. Invite the student to tell you something fun he or she did over the weekend or is planning to do soon. Use a black marker to record on paper strips exactly what the student says. Limit his or her comments to a maximum of four sentences.

2. Arrange the strips so the student can read them.

3. Model how to read the sentences using phrasing, intonation, and fluency. (You may slightly exaggerate a slower pace.)

4. Have the student read and try to mimic the same phrasing, intonation, and fluency that you modeled.

5. Reread the phrases, but stop at each phrase and cut the strips. You will now have a set of phrases.

6. Mix up the phrases.

7. Tell the student to reconstruct the sentences in proper sequence by moving the strips around. Ask the student to leave gaps between the strips so he or she can visualize the places to break when reading and train his or her eyes to see chunks of words.

8. Every time the student adds another phrase to a sentence, have him or her reread. This will provide the repeated reading in phrased chunks necessary for transfer.

9. Once the student has put together an entire sentence, he or she should have already read and reread it many times. Now the student should be able to reread the phrases with the expected phrasing, intonation, and fluency. Have the student repeat step 8 with the strips for the remaining sentences.

My mother and I

went to the aquarium

to see the dolphins.

93

Intervention Activities

Strategies: modeled phrased reading; repeated reading

Objective: Each student will be able to listen for and hear the phrased units in text and then repeat them with the same phrasing, intonation, and fluency.

Materials
- 2 tape recorders
- cassette tapes
- headset

Directions

1. In advance, have a clear, fluent adult reader read one paragraph from a classroom book and record it three times as follows:
  - Read the paragraph clearly and fluently
  - Read the paragraph one phrase at a time—stopping long enough for the student to repeat it the exact way
  - Reread the paragraph clearly and fluently.

2. Send the student to a quiet area of the room with a copy of the paragraph. Have him or her listen to the first reading. Then, have the student listen to the second reading and repeat each phrase after the speaker. Have the student listen to the third reading. Finally, have the student read aloud the paragraph on his or her own.

3. When the student understands what to do, turn on both tape recorders. Make sure that the student is following along in the book. Play the prerecorded tape on the first player. Make sure that the second player is recording.

4. Play back the tape of the student reading alone. Discuss observations related to phrasing, intonation, speed, and overall fluency.

Strategies: explicit phrasing instruction; hands-on, visual phrasing practice

Objective: Each student will be able to read the sentences by opening them up phrase by phrase. He or she will read the flip-its with increasing speed, expression, and accuracy.

Materials
- Flip-Its reproducible (page 96)
- card stock
- scissors
- envelopes
- dry erase marker or pencils

Directions

1. Photocopy the Flip-Its reproducible on card stock for each student. Cut along the solid lines. Fold back the flip-its on the dotted lines, and place them in an envelope.

2. Give one envelope to each student. Ask each student to choose one sentence from the envelope. (This allows each student to read something different so he or she does not mimic what another student says.)

3. Have the student read the phrase that is showing first and then continue to unfold the flip-it and read the next phrase. Finally, have the student reread the entire sentence with expression.

4. Monitor student reading. Use the Fantastic Five Format (page 8) for support, as needed. Have students repeat the same process with the other sentences.

Last weekend | I found a dollar

Intervention Activities

Flip-Its

Last weekend	I found a dollar	in the pocket	of my old jeans.
Our new bunny	has a bad habit	of chewing cords	and ripping carpet!
The biggest star	of the play	suddenly fell	and broke her leg!
For my birthday	I received clothes,	some new books,	and a skateboard.
Every night	before I go to bed	my older sister	reads me a story.
Her new puppy	kept her up	until late last night	crying and barking!
If my homework is done	I will go out to play baseball		with my friends.
Last summer for my vacation	I went to visit		my great grandma.
It's so hard to save money	when all I want		is to go shopping.
On rainy days	we eat lunch	in the classroom	and make a mess!
We donated money and toys	to the hospital		over the holidays.

Developing Reading Fluency • Gr. 6–8 © 2004 Creative Teaching Press